11/94

DISCIPLINE
WITHOUT
TEARS

Second Edition

DISCIPLINE WITHOUT TEARS

Rudolf Dreikurs, M.D.
and
Pearl Cassel

Featuring the
DISCIPLINE WITHOUT TEARS WORKBOOK
by David Kehoe

A PLUME BOOK

PLUME
Published by the Penguin Group
Penguin Books USA Inc., 375 Hudson Street,
New York, New York 10014, U.S.A.
Penguin Books Ltd, 27 Wrights Lane,
London W8 5TZ, England
Penguin Books Australia Ltd, Ringwood,
Victoria, Australia
Penguin Books Canada Ltd, 10 Alcorn Avenue,
Toronto, Ontario, Canada, M4V 3B2
Penguin Books (N.Z.) Ltd, 182-190 Wairau Road,
Auckland 10, New Zealand

Penguin Books Ltd, Registered Offices:
Harmondsworth, Middlesex, England

Published by Plume, an imprint of Dutton Signet,
a division of Penguin Books USA Inc. Previously published in
a Dutton Paperback Books edition.

First Plume printing, November, 1991
4 5 6 7 8 9 10 11

Contents

Kathy has deliberately dropped her pencil for the fifth time this morning. Johnny refuses to finish his arithmetic and is scribbling on his paper. Bob has just thrown a spitball across the room, while Joan has withdrawn and continues to stare blankly out of the window.

Why?

All these children have deliberately decided to behave in this way in order to find their place in the class. The methods they decided to use are based on faulty logic: and to explain the reasons for the children's actions and logic, and also how to change their behaviour, is the purpose of this book.

Many educators and teachers are confused. Some think that being permissive helps the child to express his needs and so stop the misbehaviour. Not so: what a child is really learning in a permissive class is laissez-faire anarchy, *not* democracy. He learns the philosophy of "I shall do my own thing" and "I will work only when there is something in it for me". And then we are bitterly disappointed when he openly declares his right to do anything he wants with no respect or concern for the feelings of others.

On the other hand, in very strict autocratic class-rooms, the children learn that power, prestige and profit are the only values that count. Then, on reaching adolescence, many will reject these values and rebel.

For the past 10,000 years we have lived in an autocratic society. Our children can only be understood if we first realize that the basic problem of our confused society is the rapid growth of democracy, for which we were neither trained nor prepared. This unfortunate ignorance is the crux and cause of most of the chaos in our schools.

Child rearing has always been based on tradition. Margaret Mead in her book on the South Sea Islanders describes a number of different societies, each one of them raising children a different way and bringing about different cultural patterns. In these primitive tribes, children were raised in the same manner for hundreds of generations. Both children and adults knew where they stood with each other. What is the difference between the Islanders and we North Americans? Tradition! Our traditions have changed during the past thirty years.

All living things know what to do with their young—except the parents of today. We parents and teachers must first build a new tradition, if we want to live in a world of peaceful co-existence.

This is particularly necessary in classrooms where the teacher has not been taught democratic leadership. Student fights with student, teacher fights with student; all have the mistaken belief that they can only find their place by being superior.

The old tradition of raising and teaching children, which came from an autocratic society, is no longer effective in a democratic setting. We have to learn new forms of dealing with each other because our relationships have changed. The adult/child relationships in the past were ones of dominance and submission. Today, equality is the only basis on which we'll ever be able to effectively solve discipline problems.

We are witnessing a rebellion of all those who previously were dominated in an autocratic society, and are now no longer blindly accepting the dictates of authorities. This is an unhappy yet inevitable revolution for participation in decision-making.

The desire for equality and participation was fought first in the political and legal arenas. Free men demanded to be treated equally by their legislatures and courts.

Labour was next; they didn't want to be dictated to by management. The same with the races: 'Black Power' was the war cry of the powerless. Women's Liberation was the most recent group to seek equality. Today it is our childrens' turn to fight. And just as the other groups have won, or are in the process of winning their battle for equality, so will the children. They are in the majority and they have time on their side.

Hostilities in school and home will cease only when we share the decision-making process as equals.

What is equality? It is *not* being equal in size, age, position, intelligence. It is treating each other with *equal* respect. It is having the same respect for a grade-two child as you have for your mother. It is having the same respect for your hairdresser as you have for your principal. This is the kind of equality that brings your class peaceful co-existence and makes the whole world a better place to live in.

The fundamental premises on which we should operate were formulated by Alfred Adler, a Viennese psychiatrist. His concept of the 'iron-clad logic of social living' implies the recognition of human equality. Without this recognition we will not be able to solve our conflicts and develop harmonious living . He explained the personality structure which enables us to live as free democratic men; and proposed a set of sound basic psychological premises that fit democratic principles. These can be most helpful to parents and teachers who don't know what democracy means.

His five basic premises on which to operate are:

1. Man is a social being and his main desire is to belong. This is true for adults and children alike.

2. All behaviour is purposive. One cannot understand behaviour of another person unless one knows to which goal it is directed, and it is always directed towards finding one's place. If a person or child misbehaves then it indicates that he has wrong ideas about how to be significant.

3. Man is a decision-making organism. He decides what he really wants to do, often without being aware of it. He is not a victim of forces converging on him such as heredity, environment or other outside influences, including Freud's psychosexual development. (It is the realization that man can determine what he wants to do that is the basis for our corrective and therapeutic optimism).

4. Man is a whole being who cannot be understood by some partial characteristics. The whole is greater than the sum total of the parts. (This is a very important theoretical prerequisite because it permits us to perceive the whole individual without going into a lengthy exploration. We can perceive a 'pattern' of behaviour).

5. Man does not see reality as it is, but only as **he** perceives it, and his perception may be mistaken or biased.

A teacher must understand, that if a child resists learning or misbehaves, she is not dealing with a personal maladjustment but rather with a cultural predicament.

Children are social beings who want to belong. Teachers must learn to use the group as an aid to recognize the mistaken goals of misbehaviour in children. Most adults, when correcting children only make matters worse because they do exactly what the child wants them to do— and they end up reinforcing the child's mistaken goals. Once the teacher reads this book she will understand the significance of the four goals, she can then reveal to the child what his mistaken goal is by asking him a certain sequence of questions. If this is done properly the 'recognition reflex' will follow. This indicates that the child suddenly realizes why he is misbehaving, and now alternatives are opened to him to change his behaviour.

The teacher is a group leader. She creates the atmosphere, she integrates all the diverse personalities and stimulates the democratic process. The class discussion in the classroom and the family council in the home train children in participatory democracy.

The alliance of parents, teachers and children participating in a true democracy can bring peace and harmony to our homes and schools, and ultimately to our society. The teaching profession, above all others, can use and teach democratic principles in our schools, in order to nip destructive hostilities in the bud.

Why the tears?

Presently our school system is in a dilemma regarding discipline. The controversy over punishment cannot be resolved unless we give teachers alternative effective techniques for dealing with children who misbehave and refuse to learn.

It is relatively easy to teach a class in which children want to learn, and always do the right things, but every class has at least a few youngsters who do not fit this category – and here lies the problem.

Often the teacher feels helpless and the last resort of sending a pupil to the principal's office gives the insecure teacher a certain amount of courage and confidence to face each challenging day. If teachers are to lose this privilege they must have new skills as an effective substitute action. Guidance counsellors at the junior and primary level could be most helpful to teachers in developing a preventative mental health programme. Elementary school children also need individual or group counselling when they have problems. If we wait until their troubles are big enough to take them out of our schools, or into our law courts, it is too late to redirect their early mistaken goals.

With the acceptance of the Hall-Dennis report* and other modern educational philosophies, classrooms have an ever-increasing range of ability and learning programmes. We find children are grouped for instruction yet our teachers are not trained to use group dynamics and sociometric testing. Surely the teacher must learn these skills before grouping the children for enterprise, project or creative work. Often the

* A progressive educational report published by the Ontario Government in 1967, under the title of 'Living and Learning'

pupils are confronted with social problems of working together; problems which may not have been caused by the children themselves. The teacher may not have trained them to live and learn together in a democratic setting. Traditional teaching methods where the autocratic teacher was a boss who used force, pressure, competition and a threat of punishment are now out-dated; even the pupils themselves do not accept this kind of leadership any more. If they are not given the opportunity to get involved in a participatory classroom democracy they either rebel in class, or at home, or against society in general.

Many teachers have decided to change their autocratic ways and try the democratic approach. However, because there was no one to teach them the new skills of becoming democratic leaders, they have become permissive anarchists. Their classrooms have become chaotic. Their pupils do what they want, learn what and when they want, care nothing for the needs of others, have little respect for the teacher, school or friends. Both teacher and pupil have become discouraged.

We know that when children are discouraged they misbehave, have no respect for order, and learn very little. These classrooms of laissez-faire anarchy are producing a generation of tyrants whose prime aim and value is to do their own thing with no social awareness or consideration of their responsibility to contribute to society. Permissive teachers have really abdicated their responsibility to teach. They have made the mistake of thinking that children should be allowed to learn whatever they want. Actually children should be motivated to learn what they need to learn–which in primary grades are the basic skills of reading, language and arithmetic and the social skills of living and learning in a group.

In a well organized primary classroom, where the teacher is skilled in stimulating the students to learn what they need to learn, there are few discipline problems. If the teacher believes in educating the whole child, there is ample opportunity for the development and expression of creativity through art, music, dance and the language arts. When a problem arises, the teacher immediately asks herself some questions. Was the assigned work too difficult for some, or was it too easy and consequently boring? Was the lesson preparation adequate? Was the presentation stimulating and exciting? Was it too long or too short? Have the pupils been given sufficient time to finish, and are there opportunities for fast workers to do challenging enrichment? The way in which the teacher answers these questions indicates what action she can take to improve the situation. If she is satisfied that her teaching methods are suitable, she may next go to the 'hidden curriculum' for some answers. In that hidden curriculum may live a child with a health problem, either physical or mental; a recent disappointment such as a death of a pet; or an exciting anticipation of a happy event like a birthday party. The teacher should be aware of the difference between a temporary upset and a deeper more permanent problem.

When a teacher really knows her class she is sensitive to the pupils' reactions, and if a personal problem is the cause of a disturbance she is able to offer effective guidance. However if disturbing behaviour or resistance to learning is repetitive, she can learn to diagnose the purpose of the child's mistaken goals, to understand the private logic of the child, and to redirect his behaviour.

As there are only four mistaken goals in the misbehaviour of young children, the diagnosis and treatment is fairly simple, and the methods of dealing with them will be fully explained later on. By using these methods an elementary teacher can prevent most of the personality problems that, later, trouble our high schools and our society.

Since the advent of the Hall-Dennis report, many of our junior classrooms have become less organized because it is not possible for a teacher to plan and organize work for every child at his level of development in a multi-group situation. The former degree of professional thoroughness is no longer possible when all pupils are learning a different thing at the same time. A teacher does not have the time or energy for such an idealistic structure. Teachers today need new and different methods for providing a healthy learning environment.

In open space areas, children are exposed to a variety of situations each day. They may work in small groups for basic skills, larger groups for creative experience, find themselves with a hundred others during a team teaching presentation, or alone for individual instruction. Continually making new adjustments and moving from place to place brings a series of problems. Some children cannot cope. They find it difficult to learn in this system, and they react unfavourably. Often they disturb the climate for the others. The disturbing behaviour of even one child disturbs the atmosphere of the whole class.

Within this framework, many of the old traditional values of teaching can get lost. Students may become lazy, noisy, inconsiderate and irresponsible. Work habits become sloppy, workbooks are badly written and inaccurate. We can expect a lowering of academic standards instead of the anticipated improvement. Then these students enter high school without sufficient reading skills to handle their courses. No wonder teachers are confused and discouraged. This confusion is a natural reaction to the enlightened modern educational philosophy of Hall-Dennis, and other democratic researchers of similar conviction who hoped discipline and diligence would automatically follow with the new methods of education.

Our dilemma, is that children are gaining freedom without learning an accompanying sense of responsibility.

Teachers have not been trained to teach the skills of living in a democracy. They have little knowledge of problem solving, and decision making techniques. Kurt Lewin's Iowa Experiment clearly indicates that anarchy always follows when autocratic control is lifted. Our children live in such anarchy. They reject the disciplines, ethics, ideas and values of adults; they often live in a bewildered state of idealism that lacks social interest or a satisfying sense of contribution. But there is no ill of democracy that cannot be cured by more democracy; and to begin this cure, our teachers must learn to become democratic leaders.

chapter 1

What kind of teacher are you? Autocratic or permissive

Nothing is as pathetic as a defeated authority who does not admit to that defeat.

Are you so insecure that imposing your will on children is the only way you feel you can control a class? A teacher who is committed to 'making' pupils do as they are told, forcing them to learn, berating them when they don't, punishing any misdemeanor and denying any creative freedom of expression, is an autocratic boss.

If you look down on the class, thinking how good a teacher you are in commanding children to do your will, you will sooner or later be defeated. Power, pressure and punishment to demand co-operation is the traditional approach. A teacher who uses this approach is a relic of the feudal past. This teacher imposes her ideas with a sharp voice and assumes the sole responsibility of making all decisions and rules for the class to obey.

Children today don't accept this tyrant. They 'feel' the present democratic atmosphere and expect to be treated as responsible, worthwhile, decision-making human beings. They resent being treated with scorn and react with hostility and vengeance to outwit this dominating boss. And from this lack of mutual respect they are quick to learn, firstly a double standard, and secondly, that power of any kind is of prime importance.

Some children retaliate by mockery, stubbornness, temper tantrums, disobedience, arguing or refusing to learn. As a child develops these behaviour patterns, he becomes a trouble maker, drop-out, and potential delinquent. Most of our problem teenagers today are living in an arrested state of infantile selfishness with no developed sense of responsibility toward a task, or their fellow men. To a peer group they may be loyal, but they have no respect for the young or old, or for anyone with different opinions. Many of these youngsters could have been saved by democratic teachers and counsellors; instead they have been discouraged by autocratic, insensitive bosses.

As you have been reading this, you have probably decided that you are not the tyrannical teacher who creates an atmosphere in which only a few good children become better, many bad children become worse and the majority are regulated by fear. In this type of environment the good children often strive to excel, but only to feel superior in order to look down on their classmates. They are not learning for the joy of it nor developing a willingness to meet the needs of any situation with a sense of contributing to the good of all.

Maybe you are not the autocratic tyrant who makes the bad child worse by punishing or discouraging him. Perhaps you do not have a class where there is little willing co-operation, where creativity is stifled and social and emotional growth are arrested.

But are you too permissive? Perhaps at one time you were autocratic and have now swung from one extreme to the other?

As a permissive teacher, you do not regard any child as wrong; you condone everything he does with the idea that he will turn out eventually to be a good and worthwhile member of society. You believe in providing numerous learning experiences in the classroom that pupils may choose to use. You suggest that they select their own topics or lessons for the day. You provide them with many varieties of visual aids that they may use at will. You allow them to work in groups or individually.

Some may not choose to take a reading lesson for weeks but you know they will ask you to teach them to read when they are ready. You don't really plan work for the pupils because they can learn so much more from doing research projects about things that interest them. You don't bother to give tests because they are all at different levels.

You may wonder at the end of the day what you have taught and why your head aches so much, but you know that a noisy classroom indicates that children are communicating and learning from each other. And you get disturbed when you are asked to write on a report card, or meet a parent for an interview, because you really don't have any marks or grades to help you give an accurate evaluation. In fact, you wonder if Johnny has really made any continuous progress at all, or has permanently stagnated? Perhaps you are worried to think he has even regressed?

At the end of the term, there seem to be so many materials lost or broken, so many children fighting. They disrespect the rights of others, are tired, bored, one-track-minded and unable to cope with any routine at all.

Parents are asking what is going on in your class because their youngsters seem to know less than they did last year and their behaviour at home is so uncontrollable. Several of your children are now regularly visiting counsellors, psychologists or even private psychiatrists. In general these young children are confused and don't know which end is up. They really believe they have a right to do exactly as they please and tyrannize their classmates, parents and you.

You think back, "I decided not to be an authoritarian. I read what the educational experts advised, I am a progressive teacher. But, deep in my heart, I know I really did abdicate my responsibility to teach that class, and I know most of those children could have learned to read, write and do arithmetic much better. I did not help them to solve life's problems. They cannot do meaningful project research because they cannot read the research books and I have not taught them the necessary skills. The children used to be my friends; now they disrespect me, the school, the community and even themselves. They are misbehaving because they are discouraged, and I'm discouraged too. I am very confused because I don't know what I did wrong. Shall I leave the teaching profession or tolerate my misery with resigned apathy, a drink or a tranquillizer?"

Of course this whole story is a nightmare. That permissive teacher is not really you. That teacher was a laissez-faire anarchist.

If you are not an autocrat and not an anarchist what could you be?

The only alternative is to be a good democratic leader. That is the leader who is kind but firm, who motivates pupils to learn what they ought to learn, who encourages pupils when they make mistakes, who maintains order and routine by letting each child participate in decision making.

The following are the two approaches which distinguish the autocratic leader from the democratic:

AUTOCRATIC	DEMOCRATIC
Boss	Leader
Voice, sharp	Voice, friendly
Command	Invitation
Power	Influence
Pressure	Stimulation
Demanding co-operation	Winning co-operation
I tell you what you should do	I tell you what I will do
Imposing ideas	Selling ideas
Domination	Guidance
Criticism	Encouragement
Faultfinding	Acknowledgment of achievement
Punishing	Helping
I tell you	Discussion
I decide, you obey	I suggest, and help you to decide
Sole responsibility of boss	Shared responsibility in team

The characteristic difference between the two columns is that the left indicates pressure from without, the right stimulation from within. This fundamental difference permits you to evaluate your own 'democratic index' and examine every step you take and every approach you use.

The teacher who is a democratic leader uses group dynamics, teaches responsibility by giving responsibility, and provides a mentally healthy learning atmosphere for academic, emotional and social growth for every class member, including herself.

That democratic teacher could and should be you.

chapter 2

A rewarding alternative:
teaching the democratic way

*A democratic atmosphere requires a specific
relationship as a basis for co-operation.*

Discipline is the fulcrum of education. Without discipline
both teacher and pupil become unbalanced and very little
learning takes place.

Today's discipline problems can be overcome if we turn
from the obsolete autocratic method of demanding submission and accept a new order based on the principles of freedom and responsibility. Teachers should be neither permissive nor punitive. What you have to learn is how to become
a match for your students, wise to their ways and capable of
guiding them without letting them run wild or alternately sti-
fling them.

The successful formula for guiding children in the classroom is based on the belief that democracy is not just a
political ideal, but a way of life. This freedom is not license.
It is a shared responsibility which must be taught.

You enjoy the freedoms and accept the responsibilities
of living in a democracy Before you became a teacher you
learned many skills which provided you with a freedom of
choice, and you chose to work with children. That freedom
was not license. If you had cried "I want to be free" and
your teachers had complied and not taught you skills, you
would now be shackled by your own chains of ignorance. It
is what you learn that allows you to be free.

Here is an example. Imagine that you are at a holiday
resort. The sports director suggests a variety of activities

such as swimming, tennis, badminton, water skiing, golf, sailing, dancing or bridge. Because you have been taught certain skills, you have the freedom to choose from all these activities, or you may prefer to relax and just enjoy the sun. Now think of the person who has not learned these skills. she has no choice, so really she has no freedom but to lie in the sun. She may be thinking "I wish I could swim, play tennis or golf, etc." But since she has never learned, she is actually restricted. Discipline is the seed from which freedom grows.

A person who is truly free has learned a wide variety of academic, artistic, athletic and social skills. Most of these were taught at school. By co-operation, a willingness to learn and an opportunity to exercise appropriate decision-making, this individual truly develops an ability to use free choice in any situation. Without these skills you are extremely limited and forced into a choiceless environment. We have all seen the misery caused by an individual's inability to use problem-solving techniques to make appropriate decisions, an inability that badly affects friendships and family life.

Without learned skills, courage and a sense of responsibility, you have no true freedom of choice, to work or play or to be rich or poor. Assumed freedom, without skills or responsibility, shackles man to the indignity of dependence on those who are truly free.

To be truly free means to be independent (economically and emotionally) and to use the power of self determination. Only then are you free from the control of fate, dominance and necessity.

You have experienced this kind of freedom, and from a variety of career possibilities, you have chosen to teach.

If you are a democratic teacher you will be extending your philosophy of freedom to your pupils, by assuming your role, not as an autocrat, nor as a permissive anarchist, but as a responsible guide. Your pupils will be learning skills with enthusiasm and developing social awareness by enjoying the feeling of contributing and being useful. You leave the classroom each evening confident that you have lived and learned with your pupils through an exciting, challenging day. You relax, enjoy yourself, and look forward to another day of lively experience with your pupils. Your freedom helps your students learn how to become free.

How did you reach this idyllic state? You have learned that the mental health of any teacher depends on the following six realizations:

1. You guard your physical health with periodic check-ups because you are aware that the constant effort of teaching and maintaining good interpersonal relationships requires your maximum energy. (The class of a sick teacher is sure to suffer in spite of her best efforts to be pleasant and well prepared.)

2. You like children and really enjoy teaching.

3. You understand and accept yourself with a sense of self-worth that protects you from being easily hurt or upset. You have the courage to be imperfect. You can accept criticism and even laugh at yourself sometimes.

4. You work for a sense of accomplishment and are stimulated to be imaginative.

5. You accept new challenges with confidence and courage, and always put forth a genuine effort.

6. You reserve time to take the opportunities for growth and development. Your lively interest in a number of activities, not necessarily connected with education, keeps you young and alert. Recreation in some form of play or hobby is an effective means of emotional release and self-expression. Tensions and frustrations are part of life and need to be relieved actively. It is better to swat a golf ball than a student.

You are aware of these three danger signals that may eventually cripple your mental health:

1. If you are overly anxious you may be heading for a breakdown. The burdens of anxiety and guilt develop insecurity feelings in yourself that are contagious to the children and threaten the confidence and security of a class. This can become a vicious circle with the discomfort of each aggravating the other.

2. If you are feeling desperately bored or submerged in a rut you may be dying mentally. When the life of a teacher has lost its sparkle the whole morale of the class will sag.

3. If you find yourself hating the thought of going to school every morning or feeling resentful toward your students or fellow staff members, you're applying for an ulcer. If you are feeling miserable, trying to maintain a happy expression and a tolerant attitude is a tension producing strain. Children watch for facial clues and are quicker than adults to detect insincerity. You can't fool them for long.

If you apply the following 10 points, you'll promote acceptable behaviour in a happy learning environment:

1. You are warm, friendly and kind but firm.

2. You act and speak with confidence and sincerity and express a sense of humour naturally.

3. You always have work well planned before the class starts.

4. You treat all the pupils with equal respect by

listening to their opinions and considering their feelings.

5. You are encouraging at all times, in order to develop or restore the self confidence of your pupils. By distinguishing between the deed and the doer, you never damage your relationship with the children. You may object to what a child is doing but not to the child himself. Never deny him the right to be respected as a person.

6. You are as impartial as possible. You try not to favour the pleasant likeable child or reject the one who is provocative or deficient.

7. You are able to integrate the class as a whole or divide it for group instruction in order to get optimum learning.

8. You encourage group discussion and participation in decision-making, set boundaries for expected behaviour, and maintain these boundaries with effective stimulating teaching.

9. You are not mistake centered, but always accent the positive by marking only the correct answers. You give recognition for any genuine effort.

10. You rotate the class monitors weekly, and involve all pupils in the chores and responsibilities of the classroom.

As a good democratic teacher you talk only when it is necessary and never fall into the educators trap of talking too much. You know that nagging, preaching, repeating directions and criticising is an absolute waste of 'air' time. Where discipline is concerned you know that quiet action is always more effective than words. All your pupils talk freely in controlled discussion, to develop their oral language skills, share ideas and opinions, express their creativity and plan certain class projects.

Your approaches are democratic and differ greatly from those used by the traditional autocratic teachers. You identify yourself as a group leader, not as a powerful boss. Your voice is friendly, not sharp. You win co-operation by influencing the class, rather than by demanding and using pressure. By stimulating a desire to learn, you sell ideas instead of imposing your will.

You think of guiding and helping the child, not dominating and punishing him. Every child in the class is invited to share the responsibilities of the group; you don't take on sole responsibility and demand their obedience. By offering suggestions, you help them make their own decisions. In all of these ways you stimulate from within, rather than exert pressure from without.

You occupy a crucial position in each child's life. Your influence is long lasting. After his parents, you are the first person to motivate his interest toward educational pursuits. You are responsible for setting an atmosphere in which his attitudes and achievements will grow with continuous progress.

chapter 3

How does a child grow?

Our education today is largely mistake-centered. Our children are exposed to a sequence of discouraging experiences, both at home and at school. Everyone points out what they did wrong as well as what they could do wrong. We deprive our children of the only experience which can really promote their growth and development—the experience of utilizing their own strengths.

Every child grows emotionally and socially as well as physically. There have been many charts published for teachers to describe different stages of this growth. The progression of the physical development is obvious; but we, as teachers, may be seriously trapped by concerning ourselves with a sequential approach to emotional and social growth.

Charts provide us with only an anticipation of certain behaviours and reactions, and this very anticipation may even promote such reactions that possibly the child was not intending. We teachers may be putting negative words into his mouth, or thoughts into his head. Children often behave in line with the adults expectations. Think of him as being stupid and he will sink to behave stupidly. Think of him as being mature and he will rise to meet your expectations.

Kahlil Gibran understood children perfectly when he wrote—

> Your children are not your children.
> They are the sons and daughters of Life's
>   longing for itself.
>
> You may give them your love but not your
>   thoughts,
> For they have their own thoughts.
>
> You may house their bodies but not their
>   souls,
> For their souls dwell in the house of tomor-
>   row,
> Which you cannot visit, not even in your
>   dreams,
> You may strive to be like them,
> But seek not to make them like you.

A simple yet comprehensive way of thinking of development is the three phases of childhood; life in the family before entrance to school, the elementary school days, adolescence and the entry into adult society.

In the family the child develops his own concept about himself in his transactions with parents and siblings. This forms his life style. In school he socializes in a community with children from different families. As he becomes an adolescent he is confronted with the problems of society by being most concerned with his peer group.

Basically every human, adult or child, is a social being. We all want to belong, to find our place in the group. Every action of the child is an endeavour to find this place. Some actions we accept as appropriate behaviour. If these are given recognition he will not become discouraged and switch to useless or destructive behaviour.

The child is an excellent observer but a poor interpreter. He watches all that goes on around him. He draws his own conclusions from what he sees and searches for guiding lines for his behaviour. The growing child learns to make adjustments to his inner and outer environment. The mental health of any individual depends on the adjustments that he makes and his ability to cope with problems. A child living in an encouraging environment at school can make appropriate adjustments easily. Conversely, a child in a discouraging environment, is more likely to display poor adjustments and consequently poor mental health.

The infant, only several weeks old, begins to operate on the basis of trial and error. He may even decide how he wants to be spoiled and start training his parents, who are often willing to fall for his provocations and thereby spoil him.

In Alfred Adler's early writings he discussed 'organ inferiority' which is an expression of the way in which a child responds actively to his heredity endowment. When a child is born with a certain weakness he either develops a lasting deficiency in this area, or, in order to make up for it, he develops an over-compensation and may even develop special skills in the very area where he was born with a deficiency. For example: Johnny is born with a speech impediment and later becomes an accomplished public speaker. What determined this decision? His own creativity helps him to decide. It is not the handicap which holds us back, but our attitude to that handicap. So also, a healthy child with a behaviour problem, may either over-compensate or give up.

For some years I.Q. tests have been given in public schools and the scores recorded on student record cards. Many teachers have been influenced too strongly by these possibly misleading scores, and consequently expected too much or too little achievement from their students. Our anticipation of a child's behaviour, reaction or performance often produces the actual results we expect. If we expect all children to be responsible, contributing human beings with an intrinsic worth, deserving of respect, we as teachers are more likely to find and develop that potential which is present in every growing child. As teachers of elementary school children we should be particularly aware of this growing potential. William Glasser, a successful therapist and author states:

"The critical years are between ages five and ten. Failure, which should be prevented throughout school, is most easily prevented at this time. When failure does occur, it can usually be corrected during these five years within the elementary school classrooms by teaching and educational

procedures that lead to fulfilment of the child's basic needs. The age beyond which failure is difficult to reverse may be higher or lower than ten for any one child, depending upon the community he comes from, the strength of his family, and his own genetic resources: regardless of these variations, however, it is amazing to me how constant this age seems to be. Before age ten, a good school experience can help him succeed. After age ten, it takes more than a good school experience, and unfortunately, shortly after age ten he is thrust into junior and senior high situations where he has much less chance for a corrective educational experience. Therefore, although children can be helped at any school level, the major effort should be in the elementary school."

No child is hopeless according to Adler. Any child who is told that he is a failure is deprived of his dignity and loses respect for himself.

When we are fully aware of the influence we have on each of our pupils we should think of the example that we are showing them by our own attitudes and behaviour. We should also consider the following thoughts about how a child grows according to what he lives with:

If a child lives with criticism, he learns to condemn.

If a child lives with hostility, he learns to fight.

If a child lives with ridicule, he learns to be shy.

If a child lives with fear, he learns to be apprehensive.

If a child lives with shame, he learns to feel guilty.

If a child lives with tolerance, he learns to be patient.

If a child lives with encouragement, he learns to be confident.

If a child lives with acceptance, he learns to love.

If a child lives with approval, he learns to like himself.

If a child lives with recognition, he learns it is good to have a goal.

If a child lives with honesty, he learns what truth is.

If a child lives with fairness, he learns justice.

If a child lives with security, he learns to have faith in himself and those about him.

If a child lives with friendliness, he learns the world is a nice place in which to live, to love and be loved.

chapter 4

Understanding the modern child

If training were as simple as setting a good example, we would not find so many irresponsible children coming from homes and schools where the parents and teachers are so responsible. So often, what we do to correct a child is responsible for his not improving.

Usually psychologists and psychiatrists concentrate on the children with problems and deviant behaviour, and not normal children. Sometimes we wonder, "What is really normal?" You know there are many variations of normal behaviour, and you have observed that a well adjusted normal child will display most of the following criteria.

He –

has a true sense of his own worth

has a feeling of belonging

has socially acceptable goals

meets the needs of the situation

thinks in terms of 'we' rather than just 'I'

assumes responsibility

is interested in others

respects the rights of others

is tolerant of others

co-operates with others

encourages others

is courageous

is willing to share, rather than being concerned with "How much can I get?"

is honest

puts forth genuine effort

You may be dismayed when you look at your pupils according to these ideals, but don't be discouraged: children can be trained to cultivate their innate capacity for social interest, and to develop these 'contributing' ways.

For a child to develop normally he should be encouraged by his parents, teachers, cub and brownie leaders; in fact, all adults who come into contact with a child can be either encouraging or discouraging. If an adult is discouraging, the child is very likely to have problems and to misbehave.

An Adlerian author and educator, Don C. Dinkmeyer writes:

"If you are interested in changing behaviour, whether it be in the home or the school, you must seek to establish some link between the child's already existing motives and the goals of learning. You must align what he wants to do with what he is capable of doing. Too much present motivation has been directed toward extrinsic rewards. Before children are in school any length of time, they are directed toward working for grades and other types of external evaluations.

"It is interesting to observe a class of highly spontaneous, creative, and interested kindergarten or first-grade children and then observe that same class some five or six years later when they have been subjected to the 'motivation' of grades and function mainly in response to external incentives. Ways must be found to utilize intrinsic motivation, performing for the enjoyment and satisfaction in the act, in contrast to extrinsic rewards.

When the child is directed by self-evaluation instead of external judgment, he becomes comparatively free to function. He is no longer limited by external standards."

We should realize that a misbehaving child is only a discouraged child trying to find his place; he is acting on the faulty logic that his misbehaviour will give him the social acceptance which he desires.

We should avoid criticising a misbehaving child, because our criticism just provokes hostility. A hostile child does not learn new behaviour adjustments because he uses his emotions to block his learning processes. By maintaining a friendly relationship, we can discover the child's underlying reason for the mistaken behaviour, the wrong concepts or assumptions, and then correct them.

Once we understand the goals of the child's behaviour we can practice effective methods of correction. Modifying just the behaviour is not enough; we must modify his motivation. This may be done more easily with young children and is particularly effective with preschool children. However, teachers can help all children up to the age of ten to change their goals. (But these methods are not always sufficient for the correction of older children and adolescents).

In our culture young children have few opportunities to make useful contributions toward the welfare of the family. Adults or perhaps older siblings do whatever needs to be done and the young child finds few ways to be useful and to help. It was easier for a child growing up on a farm, where there were many necessary chores to be performed, to feel that his part of the family work was a vital contribution. Nowadays, in our more affluent and urban way of life, many children make no real contribution to the welfare of others, and those who have regular chores to perform often become easily discouraged when they compare their inept performance with

CHART 1
IDENTIFYING THE GOALS OF CHILDREN'S MISBEHAVIOUR

INCREASED SOCIAL INTEREST ————→ DIMINISHED SOCIAL INTEREST

MINOR DISCOURAGEMENT ←————————→ DEEP DISCOURAGEMENT

USEFUL and SOCIALLY ACCEPTABLE BEHAVIOUR		USELESS and UNACCEPTABLE BEHAVIOUR		GOALS
Active Constructive	Passive Constructive	Active Destructive	Passive Destructive	
"success" cute remarks excellence for praise and recognition performing for attention stunts for attention being especially good being industrious being reliable (may seem to be "ideal" student, but goal is self-elevation, not co-operation)	**"charm"** excess pleasantness "model" child bright sayings exaggerated conscientiousness excess charm "Southern belle" (often are "teacher's pets")	**"nuisance"** the show off the clown walking question mark "enfant terrible" instability acts "tough" makes minor mischief	**"laziness"** bashfulness lack of ability instability lack of stamina fearfulness speech impediments untidiness self-indulgence frivolity anxiety eating difficulties performance difficulties	**GOAL 1** **ATTENTION GETTING** Seeks proof of his approval or status (almost universal in preschool children) Will cease when reprimanded or given attention
		a "rebel" argues contradicts continues forbidden acts temper tantrums bad habits untruthfulness dawdling	**"stubborn"** laziness disobedience forgetting	**GOAL 2** **POWER** Similar to destructive attention getting, but more intense. Reprimand intensifies misbehavior.
		"vicious" stealing bed-wetting violent and brutal (leader of juvenile delinquent gangs)	**"violent passivity"** sullen defiant	**GOAL 3** **REVENGE** Does things to hurt others. Makes self hated. Retaliates.
			"hopeless" stupidity (pseudo feeble minded) indolence ineptitude inferiority complex	**GOAL 4** **DISPLAY OF INADEQUACY** Assumes real or imagined deficiency to safeguard prestige.

THE WELL ADJUSTED CHILD HAS MOST OF THESE QUALITIES

Respects rights of others.
Is tolerant of others.
Is interested in others.
Co-operates with others.
Encourages others.
Is courageous.
Has a true sense of own worth.
Has a feeling of belonging.
Has socially acceptable goals.
Puts forth genuine effort.
Willing to share rather than thinking "How much can I get?"
"We" rather than "I"

This chart describes the behaviours of discouraged children up to ten years of age. Moving from Goals 4 to 3 (and so on) is a sign of improvement in the child's behaviour.

the more efficient and rapid accomplishments of adults or older siblings.

THE FOUR GOALS

After observing hundreds of misbehaving children, the senior author has identified the following as being the four goals of children's misbehaviour: attention-getting; power; revenge; and display of inadequacy.

Many attempts to discover more than these four goals have, to date, proved unsuccessful.

The four goals refer to the purpose of a child's misbehaviour. Only his actions and misbehaviour can be labeled – not the child himself.

What follows are techniques of modifying the motivation rather than the behaviour itself. When the motivation is changed, more constructive behaviour follows automatically. In order to use this 'Four Goal Technique' the following steps must be taken.

1. Observe the child's behaviour in detail.

2. Be psychologically sensitive to your own reaction.

3. Confront the child with the four goals.

4. Note the recognition reflex.

5. Apply appropriate corrective procedures.

GOAL ONE

When the child is deprived of the opportunity to gain status through his useful contributions, he usually seeks proof of his status in class through getting attention. He has the 'faulty logic' that only if people pay attention to him does he have a place in his world. But getting attention is not a way of developing his self-confidence nor does it develop self-reliance. So instead, he develops an insatiable appetite for attention and requires ever-increasing amounts of it in a misguided attempt to 'belong' and to be sure of his place.

Usually he first tries to find his place through pleasant and socially acceptable means. He may make 'cute remarks' or do stunts. Often he gives the impression of excellence and this is a source of delight to many parents and teachers. Why, then, is it called 'misbehaviour'? Because his goal is not to learn or to co-operate but rather to elevate himself to gain special attention. This maladjustment becomes apparent when praise and recognition are not forthcoming. Then the 'good' performance stops.

If the child is the 'passive' type, his methods for getting attention are of a passive nature; he is a 'model' child, a typical teacher's pet. These attributes are quite socially acceptable, especially in girls. The 'southern belle' appeals to others in her 'helplessness' and thereby gains special attention and service, with a minimum of contribution or real effort.

Attention-getting demands keep increasing. Sooner or later many children are no longer satisfied with the amounts of attention that they receive by using socially acceptable means, so they become discouraged and switch to the 'useless side'.

The active form of destructive attention-getting is labelled 'nuisance' on both charts. This includes the 'show-off' who becomes somewhat obnoxious, the 'clown' who tends to bother us, the mischiefmaker, the 'brat' who makes a nuisance of himself, and the child who keeps us constantly busy by asking questions, not for the information he receives, but to keep us occupied with him.

If the 'charm' type becomes discouraged in his first methods of passively keeping us busy, he usually switches to the useless side and becomes destructive in a passive way. We type him as 'lazy' as long as his goal is to get extra attention and service. These children manage to put others in their service by being 'inept'. They require adults to 'help' them and since children usually manage adults much better than adults manage children, the adults usually fall for their provocations. So we remind, coax, pick up after them, reassure them whenever they show fear, and act in a way which only further reaffirms their faulty evaluation of their lack of ability.

For the child who is seeking attention as his goal in life,

being ignored is intolerable. Rather than be ignored he will accept punishment, pain, humiliation, etc., in order to get the extra attention or service he yearns for. A teacher who falls for this, allows herself to be kept busy; she nags, coaxes, reminds, constantly advises and gives the child extra service. Then she feels annoyed at the child. Even if the child is using socially acceptable means of attention-getting, the teacher may at times feel that she is being kept unduly busy. By behaving in the 'natural' way, she only fortifies the misbehaving child's faulty logic and reinforces his mistaken goal.

What can she do? She should only give the child lots of attention at other times, never when he is seeking it. She should recognize that an attention-seeking child, even one who is using constructive methods, is a somewhat discouraged child. The correction of all misbehaviour is to encourage (not praise) the child. Help the child who is using destructive methods to use constructive methods, and then further encourage him to find his place by making useful contributions to the group. In other words, help the child develop his 'social interest' instead of giving him personal attention.

The shy child can be stimulated to more active behaviour by a similar procedure. Ignoring his bid for special attention through his passivity—regardless of how charming or provocative it may be—and deliberately encouraging and commenting on any **active** effort, will induce him to change his approach. This will bring out the child's best efforts without any need for attention, praise or recognition.

GOAL TWO

If parents and teachers do not employ correct methods to stop the demand for undue attention, the child becomes a power seeker. The power-seeking child wants to be the boss; he operates on the faulty logic "If you don't let me do what I want, you don't love me", or, "I only count when you do what I want you to do". In many ways the goal of power is similar to that of destructive attention-getting, but it is more intense.

The active type, labelled 'rebel' on Chart 1, often argues, contradicts, lies, may have violent temper tantrums, refuses to do what he is told to do, continues forbidden acts and may refuse to do his work—or little of it—and is openly disobedient. If he is of the passive type, his laziness is much more pronounced so that he usually does no work at all or he 'forgets', becomes stubborn and is passively disobedient.

The teacher's reaction to a power-seeking child is to feel that her leadership is threatened. She thinks "Who is running this class? He or I?" She vows "He can't get away with this: I won't let him do this to me!" But her efforts to control or force a power-drunk child are usually futile. The child will win about 99% of the time, and if she succeeds in overcoming him and defeating him, he usually becomes even more rebellious and may then seek revenge. If she wins the struggle today, he will usually win tomorrow. No final 'victory' is possible. And the longer the power struggle continues, the more the child becomes convinced that power has value, and thus his mistaken goal of finding his place is reinforced.

His 'faulty logic' seems strange to adults but it makes sense to him. He still wants to 'belong', although his methods to seek his place do not have the effect of winning friends.

What can the teacher do to help him correct his mistaken convictions? She may as well admit to him and to the class that he is a powerful person. If she fights with him, the child will win. Nobody is **obliged** to fight with a child. Many do, because they think they can win. So she should avoid getting into a power struggle with him. She should extricate herself from the conflict.

A safe way to deal with the situation would be to recognize that the power-seeking child is always ambitious and try to redirect his ambition to useful channels. He might be enlisted to help another child, or be given a position of responsibility that he feels has some prestige. (Give guidance so he won't abuse his position.) Rather than threatening him, as he anticipates, she may appeal to him for help. She may even say "I cannot make you do it and I know I can't". This may disarm him and enlist his co-operation.

An appeal to this type of child for advice and assistance will be more effective than threats. If the teacher acknowledges the child's power in his ability to defeat her, she 'takes her sail out of his wind' and there is no longer any use in his 'blowing'.

Power is only important when it is contested. Actually

we should respect a power-seeking child for the ability that he has to upset school authorities. Any child who has the teacher, principal and school psychologist all upset deserves a certain amount of credit!

GOAL THREE

If, however, the child feels so beaten down, he no longer seeks to win the power struggle, but seeks to retaliate. He uses Goal 3—Revenge.

The revenge-seeking child is so deeply discouraged that he feels that only by hurting others, as he feels hurt by them can he find his place. He views life itself and other people as grossly unfair. Convinced that he is hopelessly disliked he wants to counter-hurt. He responds with deep distrust to the teacher's efforts to convince him otherwise. And since his goal is to hurt others as he feels hurt by them, he is seemingly 'unlovable'. His actions are vicious, violent and brutal. He is openly defiant and is a potential delinquent, if not already one. He knows the vulnerability of others, whom he sees as 'opponents', and he is out to hurt them. He considers it a victory when he is labelled vicious, as this seems to be the only triumph open to him. He may injure his classmates, animals, adults; and he may scratch, bite, and kick. He is a sore loser and immediately starts plotting revenge if he is defeated, usually by even more violent methods than those used before.

Leaders of juvenile delinquent gangs are usually children who use Goal 3. They see the whole of society as their enemy and frequently look down on others with contempt. Yet underneath the facade they are deeply discouraged individuals with little hope for themselves. Usually they are active but occasionally we find one who is sullen and defiant in a 'violent passivity', and this type is even more deeply discouraged.

Children who use Goal 3 are very difficult to deal with and may require professional help, in addition to anything the teacher may be able to do. Punishment will only produce more rebellion so it is to be avoided. 'Logical consequences' (see Chapter 7) are only effective if the child really cares. The main aim of the teacher should be to try to win the child over and persaude him that he can be liked by his peers. This is difficult because much of his behaviour will deny that this is possible. The class as a group may be enlisted to help but the teacher must take steps to assure that the group will not make things worse by 'turning against' the discouraged child. 'Good' children often enlist themselves in an alliance with the teacher against the 'bad' children and this must be avoided. Group discussions may help to promote mutual understanding and help. Sometimes the teacher may enlist the help of one child who may have some empathy for the discouraged child and may be willing to be a 'buddy' to him. (see Chapter 11 for further suggestions.)

The most important thing in dealing with a revenge-seeking child, who is out to hurt the teacher, is for the teacher not to feel hurt by him.

GOAL FOUR

A child who has tried passive destructive forms of attention-getting in order to achieve the feeling of 'belonging', may eventually become so deeply discouraged that he gives up all hope of significance and expects only failure and defeat. He may actually feel hopeless or he may assume this position in order to avoid any further situation which might be embarrassing or humiliating to him. With very little self-esteem, he feels he must covetously guard what little he has. Thus he uses his inability as a protective shield to appear disabled, or to avoid any test situation in which he might lose. (He displays an inferiority complex).

His actions appear 'stupid' and he rarely participates, and by his extreme ineptitude he prevents anything being demanded or expected of him. Many children who test and behave as mentally retarded are quite capable, but so deeply discouraged that they are abandoned as 'hopeless'. They play 'stupid' successfully. Some of these may be brilliant children but use Goal 4 in a mistaken attempt to cope with a world which they view as extremely discouraging.

It is very difficult for the teacher not to fall for the child's provocation that "You can't do anything with me so leave me alone." The natural reaction is for the teacher to give up. The child's discouragement is contagious, but it is important that the teacher not yield to this provocation as she is inclined to do. Great amounts of encouragement are needed and the child must be encouraged **especially** when he makes mistakes. Every possible attempt should be made to make the discouraged child feel worthwhile. The teacher may help best by her sincere conviction that there is hope for the child and that she will not give up with him.

The teacher may be surprised to notice a child switch from one kind of misbehaviour to another. This is often a signal that the discouragement is growing worse.

The most frequent deteriorating sequence of changes which result from deepening discouragement on the child's part are:

> active-constructive attention-getting, to
> active-destructive attention-getting, to
> active-destructive power, to
> active-destructive revenge.

> **or**
> passive-constructive attention-getting, to
> passive-destructive attention-getting, to
> display of inadequacy
> (may go through a passive demonstration of power
> and sometimes, through a violent passivity revenge)

> **may also be**
> passive-constructive attention-getting, to display of inadequacy.

To recognize which goal a child is using, the teacher should understand the meaning of his behaviour. By using the accompanying charts in this chapter, teachers can become skilful in understanding the goals of children.

The younger the child the easier it is to recognize his goal in any given situation. By the time a child reaches adolescence he has learned to disguise his behaviour so that the goals are not always obvious. Also, the adolescent has other mistaken goals, such as excitement, sex, drugs, etc. Up to the age of ten the four goals prevail.

How can the teacher diagnose these mistaken goals?

Probably the most accurate clue to discovering the young child's goal is to observe your immediate response to his behaviour. Your immediate response is in line with his expectations. Thus:

If teacher feels annoyed—indicates Goal 1—Attention-getting.

If teacher feels defeated or threatened—indicates Goal 2—Power.

If teacher feels deeply hurt—indicates Goal 3—Revenge.

If teacher feels helpless—indicates Goal 4—Display of inadequacy.

Another indication is to observe the child's response to correction. If the child is seeking attention and gets it from the teacher, he will stop the misbehaviour temporarily and then probably repeat it, or something similar. If he seeks power he will refuse to stop the disturbance, or even increase it. If he seeks revenge, his response to the teacher's efforts to get him to stop will be to switch to some more violent action. A child using Goal 4 will not co-operate but will remain entirely passive and inactive.

COULD IT BE?
Once the teacher suspects the mistaken goal of the child's misbehaviour, it is most important to confront the child. The purpose of this confrontation is to disclose and confirm the mistaken goal to the child. This psychological disclosure must be done in a friendly manner, without criticism, and not at the time of conflict. The emphasis is not on 'why' but on 'for what purpose'. 'Why' implies emphasis on the past; whereas 'for what purpose' implies the child's intentions. Nothing can be done about the past, so a discussion about it is pointless and may also be inaccurate. However, the purpose in the child's present behaviour can be determined, and then his intentions may be changed while he is still in the process of constructing them.

An accurate disclosure of the child's present intentions produces a 'recognition reflex' and the facial expression is a reliable indication of his goal, even though the child may say nothing or even say 'no'. His mouth says 'no' but his nose says 'yes'. The recognition reflex is often a roguish smile, a twinkle of the eyes or the twitch of a facial muscle. Sometimes it is so open the child covers his face or bursts into laughter.

CONFRONTATION TECHNIQUES

If you were the teacher or counsellor, either in a classroom discussion period or in a private counselling situation, the conversation may go like this:

Teacher—Do you know why you did————(whatever the misbehavior was)?

Student—No. (and at an aware-level he probably honestly means it).

Teacher—Would you like to know? I have some ideas that may be helpful. Would you be willing to listen?

Student—O.K.(usually children will be interested).

Teacher—(in a nonjudgemental and unemotional way poses all the following four questions. Only one guess at a time!)

1. Could it be that you want special attention?

2. Could it be that you want your own way and hope to be boss?

3. Could it be that you want to hurt others as much as you feel hurt by them?

4. Could it be that you want to be left alone?

All four of these questions are always asked, sequentially, regardless of the child's answer or reflex because the child may be operating on more than one goal at a time. The teacher watches the body language as well as listening very carefully for the response, in order to catch the "recognition reflex". Sometimes the confrontation itself helps the child to change. The next step is for the teacher to choose and use the suggested corrective procedures. They may include using encouragement, logical consequences or finding a buddy in the same group.

Adler explains that it is not what happens to us but how we feel about it that is important. As pointed out before, all the goals of children's misbehaviour are the result of the child's 'faulty logic.' His faulty private logic is only his perception of reality.

By engaging the child in friendly conversations, by listening to his side of the story, the teacher may gain insights into ways she may help the child to correct his faulty interpretations and learn more suitable solutions. Class group discussions are also very helpful in correcting the child's faulty evaluation of situations. (See Chapter 10.)

By not falling for his provocations, by use of logical and natural consequences rather than reward and punishment, by practising mutual respect and by encouraging the child, a teacher may help him to overcome his mistaken goals and correct his behaviour.

The following Chart 2 is intended as a reference for helping you decide upon corrective procedures when facing a child with a behaviour problem. First, observe the behaviour and notice how frequently it occurs. Then, be sensitive to your own feelings or reactions to the behaviour. Check yourself and do not say or do what you feel like doing but do something else. For example, you can extricate yourself from the conflict with the child. If the child throws a temper tantrum remove yourself, or him, from the scene, quietly. Action is always more effective than words. You can also wait 'quietly' until his outburst is over. It is impossible for an enraged child to listen to anybody. He usually displays temper for the benefit of an audience. If the audience disappears, the temper often disappears too.

Only later, during the next class discussion, should you confront him with his goals. In the meantime you will have an idea of the goal he is operating on (and it may be more than one) from observing his behaviour and noting your own emotional reaction to it.

Use the advised method of confrontation asking the four "Could it be. . ." questions and watch for the recognition reflex. When you are sure of the goal, use the suggested corrective procedures from the chart. By patiently applying these methods you could see a rewarding improvement within a short time.

Even though a recognition reflex may be noticed as a response to an early question, the teacher must proceed and ask all four questions, to make sure the child is not in more than one goal.

The most discouraged child, can be trained, by an informed teacher together with a co-operative class. He can be encouraged to be happy and to learn enthusiastically, comfortable with the feeling that he really belongs to the group.

CHART 2

HOW TO CORRECT CHILDRENS MISBEHAVIOUR

BY INTERPRETATION OF THE FOUR MISTAKEN GOALS

UP TO 10 YEARS OLD

CHILD'S ACTION AND ATTITUDE	*TEACHERS REACTION	+ ASK THESE SPECIFIC QUESTIONS TO DIAGNOSE...	CORRECTIVE PROCEDURE
NUISANCE SHOW OFF CLOWN LAZY Puts others in his service keeps teacher busy Thinks "Only when people pay attention to me do I have a place"	**FEELS ANNOYED** GIVES SERVICE IS KEPT BUSY REMINDS OFTEN COAXES Thinks "He occupies too much of my time" "I wish he would not bother me"	**ATTENTION** **GOAL 1** A "Could it be that you want me to notice you?" OR B "Could it be that you want me to do something special for you?"	**NEVER GIVE ATTENTION WHEN CHILD DEMANDS IT** Ignore the misbehaving child who is bidding for attention (Punishing, nagging, giving service, advising, is attention) Do not show annoyance. Be firm. Give lots of attention at any other time.
STUBBORN ARGUES WANTS TO BE THE BOSS TEMPER TANTRUMS TELLS LIES DISOBEDIENT DOES OPPOSITE TO INSTRUCTIONS DOES LITTLE OR NO WORK Says "If you don't let me do what I want you don't love me" Thinks "I only count if you do what I want"	**FEELS DEFEATED** TEACHERS LEADERSHIP IS THREATENED Thinks "He can't do this to me" "Who is running the class? He or I?" "He can't get away with this."	**POWER** **GOAL 2** A "Could it be that you want to show me that you can do what you want and no one can stop you?" OR B "Could it be that you want to be boss?"	**DON'T FIGHT—DON'T GIVE IN** Recognise and admit that the child has power Give power in situations where child can use power productively. Avoid power struggle Extricate yourself from the conflict. Take your sails out of his wind. Ask for his aid. Respect child. Make agreement.
VICIOUS STEALS SULLEN DEFIANT Will hurt animals, peers and adults Tries to hurt as he feels hurt by others Kicks, bites, scratches Sore loser Potential delinquent Thinks "My only hope is to get even with them"	**FEELS DEEPLY HURT** OUTRAGED DISLIKES CHILD RETALIATES (CONTINUAL CONFLICT) Thinks "How mean can he be?" "How can I get even with him?"	**REVENGE** **GOAL 3** A "Could it be that you want to hurt me and the pupils in the class?" OR B "Could it be that you want to get even?"	**NEVER SAY YOU ARE HURT** Don't behave as though you are. Apply natural consequences (Punishment produces more rebellion) Do the unexpected Persuade child that he is liked. Use group encouragement. Enlist one buddy Try to convince him that he is liked.
FEELS HOPELESS "STUPID" ACTIONS INFERIORITY COMPLEX GIVES UP TRIES TO BE LEFT ALONE RARELY PARTICIPATES Says "You can't do anything with me" Thinks "I don't want anyone to know how inadequate I am"	**FEELS HELPLESS** THROWS UP HANDS DOESN'T KNOW WHAT TO DO Thinks "I don't know what to do with him." "I give up" "I can't do anything with him"	**DISPLAY OF INADEQUACY** **GOAL 4** A "Could it be that you want to be left alone?" OR B "Could it be that you feel stupid and don't want people to know?"	**ENCOURAGE WHEN HE MAKES MISTAKES.** Make him feel worthwhile. Praise him when he tries. Say "I do not give up with you." Avoid support of inferior feelings. Constructive approach. Get class co-operation with pupil helpers. Avoid discouragement yourself

* TEACHERS REACTION MUST NOT BE EXPRESSED SINCE THE 'NATURAL' REACTION IN THESE CIRCUMSTANCES WILL ONLY REINFORCE THE CHILDS MISTAKEN GOAL. EXCEPT IN GOAL 2

+ ALL FOUR QUESTIONS MUST BE ASKED OF THE CHILD IN THIS ORDER, EVEN THOUGH THE GOAL MAY BE SUSPECTED. DO NOT CHANGE WORDING.

chapter 5

Competition

*A competitive person can only stand compe-
tition when he wins. A non-competitive person will survive better in our present changing society because he is not so concerned
with what the others are doing; but with
what he himself is doing.
Competition makes a potential enemy of
every fellow man, even within the family.*

Why should we not promote competition in our junior classrooms?

Many parents want our schools to train children in the
artful sin of competitive living because they believe that such
training is necessary to prepare a young person to enter the
competitive business world. These parents do not understand
that competition for marks, grades, treats or prizes only div-
ides a class into two camps. The smaller camp being the children who learn to feel superior and look down on the large
group who do feel inferior.

There is no willing co-operation in such a school and
children do not respect each other for their individual intrinsic
worth or basic human dignity. Such children do not learn to

meet the needs of a situation, or to contribute with a healthy desire to be helpful. They do not feel that they are worthwhile because they don't feel part of the group. Their philosophy of life is 'If you can't join 'em—beat 'em!'

Only for the few with above average abilities is competition a rewarding experience. For many children it is the most discouraging method of motivating learning; they give up and regress instead of making progress.

As long as the competitive spirit is fostered, a child will waste his energies thinking about winning or losing; thereby sapping his strength and potential for the task at hand. A competitive person is conditioned through training to function only when he wins. If he loses he uses his emotions to blame others or himself, and again wastes valuable strength that could be used for realizing his full potential.

Competition is a poor excuse for those who cannot adjust to a life of equality.

A non-competitive person can function better in a competitive society because he is not concerned with what the others are doing but with what he is doing himself. And so he is free to be concerned with others as friends, neighbours and fellow human beings, rather than as competitors. This non-competitive person is not hung up with feelings of superiority or inferiority, status, prejudice or intolerance. Since he really respects himself he can treat everyone with equal mutual respect.

He has the courage to be imperfect.

With competition we cannot make a child learn or behave for long. But if we teach him democratically we can gain his co-operation and influence him for a far longer period.

These words that Alfred Adler wrote at the beginning of this century are as revolutionary now as they were then:

"Under our present system we generally find that when children first come to school they are more prepared for competition than for co-operation: and the training in competition continues throughout their schooldays. This is a disaster for the child: and it is hardly less of a disaster if he goes ahead and strains to beat the other children than if he

falls behind and gives up the struggle. In both cases he will be interested primarily in himself. It will not be his aim to contribute and help, but to secure what he can for himself. As the family should be a unit, with each member an equal part of the whole, so, too, should be the class. When they are trained in this way, children are really interested in one another, and enjoy co-operation. I have seen many 'difficult' children whose attitude was entirely changed through the interest and co-operation of fellow children.

One child in especial I may mention. He came from a home where he felt that every one was hostile to him and he expected that everyone would be hostile to him at school. His work at school had been bad, and when his parents heard of it, they punished him at home.

"This situation is only too often met with: a child gets a bad report at school and is scolded for it there: he takes it home and is punished again. One such experience is discouraging enough; to double the punishment is terrible. It is no wonder that the child remained backward and a disturbing influence in the class. At last he found a teacher who understood the circumstances and explained to the other children how this boy believed that everyone was his enemy. He enlisted their help in convincing him that they were his friends; and the whole conduct and progress of the boy improved beyond belief."

Whenever you use the democratic approach with students, rather than the competitive one, you will be amazed and delighted by the spirit of co-operation and helpfulness you receive.

In the education report 'Living and Learning' it states:

"Each and every child has the right to learn, to play, to laugh, to dream, to love, to dissent, to reach upward, and to be himself. Our children need to be treated as human beings——exquisite, complex, and elegant in their diversity. They must be made to feel that the world is waiting for their sunrise, and that their education heralds the rebirth of an 'Age of Wonder.' Then, surely, the children of tomorrow will be more flexible, more adventurous, more daring and

courageous than we are, and better equipped to search for truth, each in his own way.

chapter 6

Encouragement

A child needs encouragement like a plant needs sun and water. Unfortunately those who need encouragement most, get it the least because they behave in such a way that our reaction to them pushes them further into discouragement and rebellion.

The essence of encouragement is to increase the child's confidence in himself and to convey to him that he is good enough **as he is** not just **as he might be**.

Only when parents and teachers are encouraging does a child develop courage. Encouragement produces courage.

Undefeatable courage is the courage to be imperfect.

Too many children, and adults too, waste their potential by trying to be perfect, by thinking how good or how inadequate they are—whether they are going to succeed or fail. It is only when such thoughts are completely discarded that we can utilize our energies to meet the needs of the situation and cope with the problems that face us.

The desire to be perfect makes spontaneity and creativity almost impossible, because it chances the danger of making a mistake. How can the teacher acquire the necessary courage to be imperfect if she, in her daily routine, constantly has to watch for every infraction of perfection?

As teachers we can build on the strengths of each pupil. We should mark only correct responses instead of pointing out mistakes; then we can use those mistakes as a positive learning motivation and not as a critical evaluation of the child. If we want to find the reason for a child making a mistake, or his wrong concept and assumptions, avoid criticism. Only when we learn his true motives can we start to help him correct his misbehaviour.

We can increase every child's sense of worth if we appreciate his effort or opinion and avoid 'putting him down'. To offer this encouragement requires constant observation of the pupil's reactions. It is more than a single action. It expresses a whole process of interactions.

Encouragement is not what one says and does but how one does it. It is directed toward increasing the child's belief in himself. Only one who has faith in a child, who can see the good in him as he is, can encourage.

Children who have little self-esteem, develop a defeatist attitude, and give up when faced with anything difficult or puzzling to them.

But in an atmosphere where there is freedom and encouragement to think, combined with respect for one another, a child's confidence grows and, with it, his ability to think creatively.

Until we learn to recognize discouragement as soon as it occurs, and develop skills to help the child overcome it, we will continue to raise children who are more or less demoralized, regardless of the achievements they may have to their credit.

The moment discouragement sets in, the personality becomes warped. Regardless of how limited the area of discouragement may be, it affects a person's self-evaluation, diminishes his self-respect, renders him vulnerable, and makes him timid and fearful. We need courage to meet the tasks of life and to fulfil our potential. Discouragement drains a person's strength and courage.

No child would switch to the socially unacceptable side of life if he were not discouraged. He believes that he has no place in the group and can't succeed with useful means, therefore he is discouraged,—and the terrible circle is continued. Democratic teachers have the power to break that vicious circle.

When we discourage a child we quell the ecstasy of learning. Albert Einstein explained why he was unable to think about scientific problems for a year after his final exams. He said:

"It is in fact nothing short of a miracle that the modern methods of instruction have not yet entirely strangled the holy curiosity of inquiry.... It is a very grave mistake to think that the enjoyment of seeing and searching can be promoted by means of coercion and a sense of duty."

And yet, life and joy cannot be subdued. The blade of grass shatters the concrete. The spring flowers bloom in Hiroshima. An Einstein emerges from the academies. Those who would reduce, control and quell must lose in the end because the ecstatic forces of life, growth and change are too numerous, too various, and too tumultuous.

To nurture these ecstatic forces of life we may use some of the following 20 points to encourage every student who looks to us for guidance:

1. Avoid discouragement—because the feelings of inferiority which all humans experience in one form or another, must be overcome if we are to function well.

2. Work for improvement, not perfection.

3. Commend effort.
   One's effort is more significant than one's results.

4. Separate the **deed** from the **doer**:
   One may reject the child's actions without rejecting the child.

5. Build on strengths, not on weaknesses.
   A misbehaving child has the power to defeat the adult. Give him credit for this.

6. Show your faith in the child.
   This must be sincere, so one must first learn to trust the child.

7. Mistakes should not be viewed as failures.
   We need to take away the stigma of failure.

Failure usually indicates lack of skill. One's worth is not dependent on success.

8. Failure and defeat will only stimulate special effort when there remains the hope of eventual success. They do not stimulate a deeply discouraged child who has lost all hope of succeeding.

9. Stimulate and lead the child, but do not try to push him ahead. Let him move at his own speed.

10. Remember that genuine happiness comes from self-sufficiency: children need to learn to take care of themselves.

11. Integrate the child into the group.
Treating the child as 'something special' increases his over-ambition. An over-ambitious child who cannot succeed usually switches to the useless side of life with the 'private logic': "If I can't be best, I'll at least be the worst." Even more serious, he may give up altogether.

12. Stimulating competition usually does not encourage children.
Those who see hope of winning may put forth extra effort, but the stress is on winning rather than on co-operation and contribution. The less competitive one is, the better one is able to withstand competition.

13. Praise is not the same as encouragement.
Praise may have an encouraging effect on some children, but it often discourages and causes anxiety and fear. Some come to depend on praise and will perform only for recognition in ever-increasing amounts. Success accompanied

by special praise for the result may make the child fear "I can never do it again!"

14. Success is a by-product.
Preoccupation with the obligation to succeed is intimidating and the resulting fear and anxiety often contribute to failure. If one functions with the emphasis on what contribution he may make or how he may co-operate with others, success usually results.

15. Help the child develop the courage to be imperfect.
We should learn from our mistakes and take them in our stride.

16. Don't give responsibility and significance only to those who are already responsible.
Giving opportunities to be responsible to a child who is discouraged may make it worth while for him to co-operate.

17. Solicit the help of other members of the class to help a discouraged child find his place in useful ways.

18. Remember that discouragement is contagious. A discouraged child tends to discourage his teacher.

19. Avoid trying to mend one's own threatened ego by discouraging others or by looking down on them.

20. Overcome your own pessimism and develop an optimistic approach to life. Optimism is contagious—it not only encourages you but those around you.

Many teachers feel that encouragement is the same as praise. This is not true; there's a subtle difference between the two. Praise is only needed by a very few children in order to stimulate them into right behaviour. The satisfaction of doing a job well is reward enough.

We should recognise the perfect worker occasionally. The remarks "Well done!" or "Keep up the good work" are adequate. We must be careful never to imply that his personal worth depends only on his accuracy.

Encouragement however, is needed by all children; particularly when they make mistakes. Encouragement is often difficult for the adult to express, and it takes practice.

If we watch a child closely when he is receiving praise we may discover some astonishing facts. Some children gloat, some panic, some express "so what," some seem to say, "Well, finally!"

We are suddenly confronted with the fact that we need to see how the **child** interprets what is going on rather than assume that he regards everything as **we** do.

Examination of the intention of the praiser shows that he is offering a reward. "If you are good you will have the reward of being high in my esteem." Well, fine. What is wrong with this approach? Why not help the child learn to do the right thing by earning a high place in teachers' esteem?

But if we look at the situation from the child's point of view, we will find the mistake of this approach.

How does praise affect the child's self-image? He may get the impression that his personal worth depends upon how he 'measures up' to the demands and values of others. "If I am praised, my personal worth is high. If I am scolded, I am bad. If I am ignored, I am worthless."

When this child becomes an adult, his effectiveness, his ability to function, his capacity to cope with life's tasks, will depend entirely upon his estimation of how he stands in the opinion of others. He will live constantly on an elevator of happiness—up and down, frequently with someone else pushing the button.

Praise is apt to center the attention of the child upon himself. "How do I measure up?" rather than "What does this situation need?" This gives rise to a fictive-goal of "self-being-praised" instead of the reality-goal of "what-can-I-do-to-help?"

Another child may come to see praise as his right. Therefore, life is unfair if he doesn't receive praise for every effort. "Poor me—no one appreciates me." Or, he may feel no obligation to perform if no praise is forthcoming. "What's in it for me? What will I get out of it? If no praise (reward) is forthcoming, why should I bother?"

Praise can be terribly discouraging. If the child's efforts fail to bring the desired amount of praise he may assume either that he isn't good enough or that what he has to offer isn't worth the effort and so he gives up.

If a child has set exceedingly high standards for himself, praise may sound like mockery or scorn, especially when his efforts fail to measure up to his own standards. In such a child, praise only serves to increase his anger with himself and his resentment at others for not understanding his dilemma.

In all our efforts to encourage children we must be alert to the child's response. The accent must move from "You are good" to "How you have helped in the total situation." Anything we do which reinforces a child's false image of himself is discouraging. Whatever we do that helps a child see that he is an important part of a functioning unit, that he can contribute, co-operate, participate within the total situation, is encouragement. We must learn to see that as he is, the child is acceptable, even though his work may not be.

Praise rewards the individual and tends to fasten his attention upon himself. Little satisfaction or self-fullfilment comes from this direction.

Encouragement stimulates the effort and fastens attention upon one's capacity to join humanity, and also to become aware of interior strength and ability to cope.

Praise recognizes the actor, encouragement acknowledges the act.

The following chart stresses this crucial difference between praise and encouragement. The sentences under praise are **not** encouraging but produce a false superior self-awareness.

PRAISE	ENCOURAGEMENT
Aren't you wonderful to be able to do this!	Isn't it nice that you can help? We appreciate your help. How tidy our class room looks now. Thanks for comforting Susan. It was a big help. I like your drawing. The colours are so pretty together. How much neater your desk looks now that your books are put away. How nice that you could figure that out for yourself. Your skill is growing!
I'm so proud of you for getting good grades. (You are high in my esteem.)	I'm so glad you enjoy learning. (adding to your own resources)
I'm proud of you for behaving so nicely on the school bus.	We all enjoyed being together on the school bus.
I'm awfully proud of your performance in the recital.	It is good to see that you are enjoying playing the instrument. We all appreciate the job you did. I give you credit for working hard.

As we work with children we very quickly learn that our tone of voice can be of major importance. The same sentence can be spoken in an encouraging or discouraging way, depending on our attitude to the child or class.

The following remarks are suggestions that will be encouraging to a child but they will work only if you express a feeling of trust, confidence, acceptance and belief in that child. If you express a feeling of moralizing, preaching, or impatience, these same suggestions will have discouraging results:

1. "You do a good job of . . ."
   Children should be encouraged when they do not expect it, when they are not asking for it. It is possible to point out some useful act or contribution in each child. Even a comment about something small and insignificant to us may have great importance to a child.

2. "You have improved in . . . ."
   Growth and improvement is something we should expect from all children. They may not be where we would like them to be, but if there is progress, there is less chance for discouragement. If they can see some improvement, children will usually continue to try.

3. "We like (enjoy) you, but we don't like what you do."
   After a child makes a mistake or misbehaves, he often feels he is not liked. A child should never think **he** is not liked. It is important to distinguish between the child and his behaviour, between the act and the actor.

4. "You can help me (us, the others, etc.) by . . . ."
   To feel useful and helpful is important to everyone. Children want to be helpful; we have to give them the opportunity.

5. "Let's try it together."
   Children who think they have to do things perfectly, are often afraid to attempt something alone or new, for fear of making a mistake or failing. They are likely to feel more secure with a group project.

6. "So you made a mistake? Now, what can you learn from your mistake?"
   There is nothing that can be done about what has happened, but a person can always do something about the future. Mistakes can teach the child a great deal, and he will learn if he is not made to feel embarrassed for having made one.

7. "You would like us to think you can't do it, but we think you can."
   This approach could be used when the child says or conveys that something is too difficult for him. But if he tries and fails, he has at least had the courage to try. Our expectations should be consistent with the child's ability and maturity.

8. "Keep trying. Don't give up."
   When a child is trying, but not meeting much success, a comment like this might be helpful.

9. "I'm sure you can straighten this out, (solve this problem, etc.) but if you need any help, you know where to find me."
   Teachers need to express confidence that children are able to resolve their own conflicts.

10. "I can understand how you feel (not sympathy; but empathy) but I'm sure you'll be able to handle it."
    Sympathizing with another person seldom helps him, rather it conveys that life has been unfair to him. Understanding the situation (empathizing) and believing in the child's ability to adjust to it is of much greater help.

All that has been suggested in this chapter is crucial to the intricate process of education. Success breeds fulfilment, self-acceptance, and the belief that one can achieve. Frustration and discouragement lead to suppressed aggression or to aggressive action, conflict and deviant behaviour.

It is only when the child understands himself, his needs, purposes and attitudes and develops an awareness of how to relate to others that he is freed to become involved in the educative process.

This process can be idealized in the following philosophy:

To learn joyously and enthusiastically.

To learn co-operation for the well-being of society.

To learn discipline by stimulation from within.

To learn responsibility by being given responsibility.

To learn empathy for others by becoming sensitive to them.

To learn a sense of security that comes from the faith that we can cope with the insecurity of life.

To learn self-esteem by living without shame or guilt.

To learn to like oneself, by feeling accepted as one is.

To learn to love and grow by living with friendship and acceptance.

To learn commonly-agreed upon knowledge and skills of the ongoing culture.

To learn to reason and make decisions by participating in decision making.

To learn appreciation by respecting the contribution each person makes.

To learn confidence by living with encouragement.

chapter 7

Logical consequences, not punishment

Punishment is only effective for those who don't need it.

When the teacher punishes; the child's reaction is "If the teacher has the right to punish me, I have the same right to punish her." This is a major reason why our classrooms are filled with acts of retaliation.

Herbert Spencer, about one hundred years ago, pointed to the ineffectiveness of punishment in a democratic setting and distinguished between punishment and natural consequences. Piaget extended this concept by distinguishing between retributive justice, which is punishment, and distributive justice, which is the power and force of reality and of the social group.

Yet the vast majority of teachers still expect good results from a method which at best, brings temporary compliance. Punishment does not influence behaviour or 'teach' anything today.

You may believe that reward and punishment are essential for the rearing and teaching of children. Many share that belief. But, reward and punishment have detrimental effects on the development of the child particularly in the democratic atmosphere that prevails today. Only in an autocratic society are they an effective and necessary means of obtaining conformity; they pre-suppose a certain person is endowed with superior authority. In a democracy, a status of social equality is granted to everybody, and the authority of one over others is refuted. This is difficult to accept, especially in a classroom.

In a democratic atmosphere the 'control' of parents and teachers over children diminishes. Outside pressures on the child can no longer 'make' the child perform. The child reacts to rewards by regarding them as his 'right', refusing to do his share unless he gets one. Conversely, if the child is punished, he feels that he has the same right to punish the adults.

If you want to influence the development of children you will find that the methods suggested in this book fit into the new democratic era. First, the principle of reward and punishment must be abandoned. But this does not mean embracing a 'permissive' attitude; this would only create chaos and anarchy. Instead choose democratic methods which are based on the recognition of mutual equality, mutual respect, and order in the classroom.

In a system of mutual respect a job is done because it needs doing and the satisfaction comes from the harmony of two or more people doing a job together. Children don't need bribes to be good. They actually **want** to be good. Good behaviour on the part of the child springs from his desire to belong, to contribute usefully and to co-operate.

When we bribe a child for good behaviour we are, in effect, showing him that we do not trust him, which is a form of discouragement. The system of rewarding children for good behaviour is as detrimental as the system of punishment. There is no reward that totally satisfies.

True satisfaction comes from a sense of contribution and participation. Children who are trained to be competitive only feel worthwhile when they are on top or superior. If they don't win they feel unhappy and inferior. Children trained in an atmosphere of co-operation know that by merely existing they are an accepted part of humanity.

Some teachers believe that, without punishment, or threat of it, children will not conform or perform. Some even say that the only way of maintaining discipline is by using a strap.

But all recent research in education and child-adult relationships finds that punishment is, at best, only a temporary deterrent to repeated misbehaviour. (In Behaviour Modification the reward is a temporary crutch.) The teacher who does the punishing may feel a sense of satisfaction herself, but as a training device the actual punishment is useless. You may ask, "How can I train a child without the threat of punishment?"

The most effective training devices are an outcome of the understanding that man is basically co-operative—not competitive. As Desmond Morris states:

"If we did not carry in us the basic biological urge to co-operate with our fellow men, we would never have survived as a species. If our hunting ancestors had been competitive, ruthless, greedy tyrants, the human success story would have petered out long ago."

The democratic teacher uses not punishment but natural and logical consequences. Punishment invites retaliation and is not an effective teaching method. **Logical** consequences, structured and arranged by the adult, must be experienced by the child as logical in nature. He will see the consequence of his behaviour by experience and will learn from it. However, logical consequences should never be used in a power struggle . . . they may backfire.

Natural consequences are based on the natural flow of events and are those which take place without adult interference. These are the best training techniques.

> We want to convey to the child that he is able to take care of his problem, not that he must do what we decide.

> We should not assume responsibilities for children nor should we take the consequences of their actions.

> We have no **right** to impose our wills on children. However, we do have an obligation not to give in to children's undue demands.

We have no **right**, in a democratic society, to punish.

We have an obligation to guide. Democracy requires leadership.

We can no longer force proper behaviour; we can only stimulate appropriate behaviour.

In applying logical consequences, do not remind, threaten, coax, or talk too much.

If logical consequences are used as a threat or 'imposed' in anger, they become punishment.

Avoid using logical consequences as disguised punishment.

There is not always a natural consequence or a logical consequence for every situation. However, when adults tend to think in these terms, their own creativity will increase, and appropriate means may more often be found.

Ask yourself "What would happen if I didn't interfere?"

Logical consequences are an effective corrective procedure for children displaying Goal 1 behaviour. For Goals 2 and 3, only natural consequences should be used. In Goal 4 do not use either.

LOGICAL CONSEQUENCES	PUNISHMENT
A learning process.	A judicial proceeding.
Adult plays the role of an educator.	Adult plays the role of policeman, judge and jailer.
Adult is understanding, sympathetic.	Adult is usually angry.
Adult is interested in the situation and its outcome.	Adult is interested in retaliation.
Adult tries to be objective, with little emotional involvement.	Adult often is subjective, with considerable emotional involvement.
Express the reality of the social order, not of the person.	Expresses the power of a personal authority.
Are intrinsically related to misbehaviour.	Has an arbitrary connection to misbehaviour and its consequences.
Have no element of moral judgment.	Inevitably involves some moral judgment.
Are concerned with what will happen now.	Is concerned with the past.
Give the child a choice of his behaviour and the results.	Gives no choice to the child.
Respect the child.	Belittles or demeans the child.
Distinguish between the **deed** and the **doer**.	Denotes sin.

Child is accepted, although his behaviour is not.	Implies that the child has no value.
Is firm but fair.	Is often unfair.
Voice is calm and friendly.	Voice is loud and angry.
Is appropriate in a democratic setting	Belongs only in an autocratic setting.

Many of the great philosophers and educators believed that punishment was useless for improving human behaviour. In the late nineteenth century Nietzsche wrote, "Punishment hardens and numbs, it sharpens the consciousness of alienation, it strengthens the power of resistance."

By using consequences instead of punishment, the teacher allows reality to replace the authority of the adult. It is not easy to separate consequences from punishment; often the only difference is the teacher's tone of voice and attitude toward the child. The teacher may say, "You will see what happens" to prepare the child for the natural consequences. But the same words shouted, or said as a threat, can imply punishment. Consequences permit the child to decide what he can and wants to do about the situation.

What does a teacher often do when she is confronted with a noisy class? She adds her noise to that of the pupils. Instead, she could soften her voice or stop talking altogether. The children will see to it that the class will be quiet. It is essential that the teacher acts like a bystander, helping a child to respond to the demands of the situation rather than to her personal demands. As soon as the teacher gets upset, she becomes personally involved and turns the best consequence into a futile punitive act.

Here is an example of resolving a problem without fighting or losing face:

A kindergarten child always refused to come into the classroom unless coaxed. One day the teacher decided not to give him special attention but gave him the choice to stay out or come in. When he saw that the first period was play and fun, he decided to join in. After that he entered the classroom each day by himself.

If a child is not listening in a reading lesson the logical consequence would be to let him miss his turn for oral reading. Most children like to read aloud because it gives them the opportunity for centre stage. This consequence will help train the child to become more careful and attentive.

If a whole class of young children is inattentive, the teacher can go to the back of the room and work at her desk. She may say, "Children, when you are ready you can ask me to teach you." It is surprising how often the class elect a spokesman to appeal to the teacher. This is less effective with older children and not advisable unless the class has had some democratic training.

A little boy misbehaved by continually falling off his tipped chair. The teacher removed the chair, without saying a word, and he had to stand. By the quiet action she avoided the power conflict. She impressed the child. If she had scolded him, the other pupils may have followed his example and he would have repeated it. Silent action by a teacher is always more effective than words.

A teacher cannot apply consequences when she is angry or upset. They must be a logical or natural outcome of a series of events. An imaginative teacher can think of many different logical consequences that will be effective in promoting co-operative rather than competitive behaviour. Teaching a class in a democratic atmosphere is always a pleasure.

chapter 8

Conflict solving and how to deal with tyrants

The key words for both conflict solving and dealing with tyrants are 'mutual respect'. In the human relationship between a teacher and child this respect for the child involves an attitude of kindness but firmness. The first expressing respect for the child, the second, respect for oneself.

A 5-year old boy shouted, "Miss Jones who's boss around here—you or me?"

You may dismiss this as a cute remark but let's look at what is really happening. Since children have been exposed to all kinds of media they are demanding their rights, like any other minority group. No longer does the child consider himself inferior and the adult superior.

We as teachers must recognize that each child is a unique, dignified human being, and have respect for him at all times. Then a feeling of mutual trust can be established. And only in such a situation are teachers able to be really effective in their relationships with students.

By the time a modern child is six or seven years old, he has an expansive awareness from constant exposure to mass media; the prime contributor being TV. But we must remember that although a child is an excellent observer, he is a very poor interpreter, and needs someone to put his observation in proper perspective.

This involves empathy, listening to the child, trying to understand, and helping him by showing him the decision-making process. If this is not done, these young children become 'little tyrants' and eventually grow into very big tyrants who dominate and humiliate their wives, husbands, children, co-workers and neighbours.

Little tyrants tyrannize their parents, playmates, neighbours, group leaders, classmates and teachers. Many have this behaviour pattern well established before they leave the play-pen.

Since you are a democratic teacher you can recognize and deal with these children by applying some principles and skills of conflict-solving. Fighting or giving in is no solution. Many teachers do not realize that anyone who fights with a child is bound to lose in the long run because the child is a smart manipulator, and the teacher is no match for him.

Most people in conflict situations think that they can make the other person change by using words; and teachers who want to force a child often fall into the same trap. Words are supposed to be a means of communication; but in a conflict situation the child is unwilling to listen, and the words become weapons. When a child is in a temper tantrum it is useless to talk to him. Waiting quietly until the temper is over, or quietly but firmly removing him, is far more effective. In fact talking to him is the worst possible procedure because it is probably exactly what the child wants, and the teacher is simply falling for his mistaken goal.

Wherever people live conflicts are inevitable because of differences of opinions, interests and goals. This is particularly true of the group life of a teacher with children in a classroom. In the past conflicts were resolved by the person or group in power. The teacher represented this power and was able to exert her authority to make children behave. But in a democratic setting, nobody is willing to accept imposition and defeat. Today, children resist this kind of autocratic force. Teachers try to tyrannize children and children try to tyrannize teachers and both suffer from the inability to get along with each other.

Actually, if you know how to deal with conflicts, you will

find that teaching is really a rewarding and enjoyable profession. Here is a typical classroom problem:

Johnny is refusing to do his work and is disturbing the class. What does the teacher usually do in this situation?

First, she protests and tells him how wrong he is, and then, because he is so stubborn, she wearily gives in. The correct solution is to do the exact opposite.

If the tyrant demands and argues, first, you simply reply "You may have a point." Second, you do whatever **you** think is right. He cannot continue acting the tyrant unless you agree to stay and fight with him. If you do stay to try and convince him to conform you will only get yourself involved in a losing battle. Do not fall into the trap of thinking, "I must stay and resolve this problem because my personal status is at stake." The misbehaving child and the rest of the class will not consider you a coward if you don't win a clear cut victory. You will not lose dignity; the class will respect you as a wise diplomat who can resolve the major conflict by sidestepping a battle.

No one gains anything by fighting or giving in, but most of us when confronted by a tyrant, either adult or child, usually do fight and eventually give in. And when the pupil is the tyrant, he will almost always be able to force the teacher to do what he wants. Most teachers are blind to this fact of classroom life.

A teacher who understands the four goals of misbehaving children will be more able to cope with a conflict situation, and realize that the conflict may be instigated by the child but perpetuated by the teacher.

In a democratic setting, nobody is willing to accept imposition and defeat; every victory is short lived. The techniques by which conflicts can be resolved in a democratic setting were well established by Adler 40 years ago but are little known today.

Teachers have to learn to influence children rather than to coerce them. We can use social pressures in a democratic classroom by sociometric testing and by the use of group dynamics. Mutual respect is a pre-requisite to solving conflict situations. The following are four principles that can help in producing harmony. They were only recently formulated as a basis for conflict-solving in a democratic setting, in the class-room or anywhere else where conflict exists.

> **1. Don't fight, Don't give in**. When you fight, you violate respect for the child. When you give in, you violate respect for yourself.

> **2.** One must **identify the nature of the conflict**. It is hardly ever the issue about which disagreement exists; it is usually the teacher's personal involvement, concern with status, with winning or losing, with vanity, ambition or other personal goals.

With children under ten years the goals of misbehaviour are easier to define as previously described. With teenagers it is more complicated because other goals, like excitement, daring and sex—all recognized and promoted by the peer group—are involved in the conflict. The goal of peer acceptance is a strong motivator. In adults the goals of profit, power and prestige are often active ingredients in any fight.

A teacher who can understand and identify the underlying cause of the conflict is moving toward a peaceful and co-operative class.

> **3.** Reach agreement on what you want to do. We always want the **other** one to change. The only one who can freely change is you. When you change, then the whole relationship is changed. **Extricating yourself** is the first step in changing the agreement between teacher and child.

When two people fight they have made an agreement to do so. In order to have a fight one must first communicate the desire and then find co-operation with the antagonist. Everything we do with other people, including fighting, involves mutual co-operation.

Only when one stops and thinks, "What can **I** do about this hostile situation?" can the conflict be resolved. Thinking only of what the opponent should do, leaves no room for understanding, and nothing can be changed.

One must reach agreement. Few people consider this possible in a conflict situation. Actually, whatever happens in a relationship, it is based on agreement, communication and full participation. If one changes one's own role, a new agreement is inevitable. One usually thinks only of what the opponent should do—instead of thinking what one could do oneself.

> **4. Let everybody in the conflict participate in the decision-making:** As soon as the child learns to talk, we should listen to him ... we need democratic leadership which neither fights nor gives in but integrates.

Conflicts cannot be resolved without shared responsibility, without full participation in decision-making of all the participants in a conflict. Democracy does not mean that everybody can do as he pleases. It requires leadership to integrate and to win mutual consent.

In the following chapter you will find that during the weekly discussion period all the pupils take part in the decision-making process. This scheduled time for discussing problems eliminates most of the conflicts that happen from day to day. But when these conflicts between teacher and child do occur remember the following points.

Respect the other person

Don't fight, don't give in

Pinpoint the issue

Change the agreement.

When attempting to solve any conflict we must realize that in order to change the attitude of our opponents we must first change our own attitude toward them. The secret is, in changing ourselves; the change in them will automatically follow. Don't push; pull! If we step aside and leave space, our antagonist will have room to move over to our position.

In all human relationship problems the key words are mutual respect. Even a tyrant of the worst kind, old or young, deserves our respect by virtue of his mere humanity. In fact many tyrants, because they are so insecure, appreciate our respect very deeply.

Dr. F. J. C. Seymour, Assistant General Secretary of the Alberta Teachers' Association, gives the following suggestions to help resolve arguments:

1. *Don't lose your temper, you'll lose your point.*
2. *Remember, you are trying to win an agreement, not an argument.*
3. *Apologize when you're wrong, even on a minor matter.*
4. *Don't imply superior knowledge or power.*
5. *Acknowledge with grace the significance of the other's comment or statement of fact.*
6. *Know and admit the impact of your demands.*
7. *Remember that the ability to separate fact from opinion is the mark of a clear mind and reflects intellectual integrity.*
8. *Stay with your point: pursue your objective but don't devastate.*
9. *Don't quibble: say what you mean and mean what you say. If you want truth, give it.*
10. *Bargain in good faith. Your intellect will tell you when you're bargaining and your conscience will tell you whether you have good faith.*

As long as we regard tyrants as monsters they will behave accordingly. On the other hand, if we respect them as human beings with an honest expression of equality, without giving in, then we are more likely to live with tyrants peacefully and perhaps change their attitude to one of co-operation.

chapter 9

Is your class a group?

Do you regard your class as a mirror of your own personality, feeling confident only when they obey and inadequate when they disturb? Or do you really feel that you belong to your class as a group member?

It is unfortunate that we spend more time struggling against an untrained child than we spend in training him to socialize in the life of a group. In the previous chapters we have learned **what** makes a child tick; now we will find out **how** a child ticks (in a group).

We suffer from a deep unrecognized prejudice toward children. We fail to recognize their strengths or capacities.

Most teachers assume that they single-handedly have to teach and to correct a given number of children in their class, be it large or small. But if the teacher knows how to be a group leader, it should make little difference whether there are 10, 30 or 50 children, because it is still only one class.

We need special skills to utilize group dynamics and to create a group atmosphere in which all students become willing and able to learn, as one cohesive and co-operative group. This does not necessarily mean homogeneous in age or ability.

As we use teaching methods such as the Joplin Plan and The Open Space concept, we find it increasingly important to integrate the pupils either as classes or for certain periods each day. In fact, if we don't make an effort towards this integration, we soon find that any class is split between those who are with us and those who are against us.

SOCIOMETRIC TEST

A sociometric test can be useful to help the enthusiastic teacher understand and integrate sub-groups in her class; to integrate the isolate, and to improve the relationships and social interaction. The results of such a test can influence the seating plan in the classroom, the grouping of students for projects or enterprises, the formation of committees, and the understanding of cliques and leaders.

But before giving the test, observe the following precautions:

1. Members of the group should know each other rather well.

2. The entire process should be completed as casually as possible.

3. Pupils must feel that the information will be treated with confidence.

4. Pupils must feel that the teacher is trying to help.

5. The word 'test' should be avoided; its use may cause some pupils to give the 'right' answers rather than the 'correct' ones.

6. Clear questions must be asked.

7. Questions must apply to only one situation and the pupils must understand this.

8. Pupils must understand how the results are to be used.

9. The results should be used as soon as possible and the pupils should be aware that they are being used.

Bearing in mind that the purpose of the test is two-fold—diagnostic, and as a basis for changes in relationships—the questions asked must be meaningful and well within the realms of reality for every student. The questions may be:

> **1.** Name three pupils in the class that you would like to sit with.
> (a) If there is one person that you would prefer not to sit with, name that person. You may leave this question unanswered if that is your choice.
>
> **2.** Name three pupils in the class that you enjoy playing with in the yard.
> (a) If there is one person that you would prefer not to play with, name that person. You may also leave this question unanswered.
>
> **3.** In working on a group project name three people that you would like to work with.
> (a) If there is one person that you would prefer not to work with, name that person. You may leave this question unanswered.

From these six questions you will get sufficient information to see a clear picture of the group dynamics operating within the class. On the following page you will find a description of how to summarize this information graphically.

Sociometric Test Results

To summarize the data from a matrix and point them up more graphically, the target method is useful. To construct a target, draw four concentric circles as shown below.

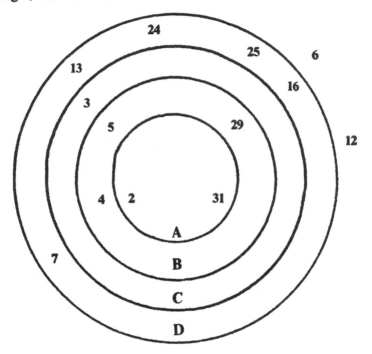

First, give each child a number. Then in the centre circle, A, the bull's-eye, place the numbers of the pupils who receive more positive choices than would occur if the choices were evenly distributed among all the pupils. If each pupil is asked to choose three others he likes, an even distribution would give each pupil three votes. In this case pupils who receive four or more positive choices, and no negative choices, are placed in the bull's-eye.

In ring D, place the numbers of those pupils who receive four or more negative choices or rejections and one or no positive choices. In ring B, place the numbers of those who are more liked than disliked, even though they are not highly chosen. In ring C, place the numbers of those who are more disliked than liked. Place the numbers of the neglected pupils outside the target area.

You may be thinking "Now that I have this information what do I do with it?"

For group project work it is more profitable to put compatible pupils together. They will contribute to the task with the least friction.

The isolates can be encouraged to join an extroverted group where new skills in socialization may be experienced, or a buddy system can be set up by the teacher with **volunteers** from the class. In the playground the teacher can deliberately steer the isolate toward group games by giving him the class ball or any other piece of sports equipment.

The seating plan of the classroom can be re-arranged to accommodate the preferences of the pupils. Of course, if discipline problems do arise from friends talking together instead of working, you will need to change the seating plan again. But don't anticipate trouble; usually the pupils appreciate recognition of their request and co-operate as a sign of gratitude. They like to be near their friends and appreciate a teacher who shows this kind of understanding.

It is interesting to repeat the sociometric test procedure two or three times a year in order to find out what new relationships have been established and hopefully to eventually have no isolates at all. This is a realistic aim as a class moves toward co-operative cohesion.

chapter 10

The class discussion period

We can teach responsibility only by giving the pupils opportunities to accept responsibilities themselves.

It is important to remember that any problem child is a problem for the whole class, and the solution to the problem grows most naturally out of the helpful involvement of all class members.

If the teacher uses the co-operation of the pupils instead of her own authority for behaviour correction, there will be many advantages for all. The discouraged or misbehaving child will begin to feel that he belongs to the group. This reduces his discouragement and stimulates him to change his behaviour. The class members feel less frustrated about a miserable situation and enjoy the opportunity to contribute to its improvement. They learn to think positively about the discouraged child and become more tolerant human beings. Their prejudices are nipped in the bud. They learn to express constructive ideas and feel a sense of satisfaction when they are accepted by the group.

From the teacher's quiet but concerned action they learn that there are other methods of solving personality differences, without fighting. The teacher has extricated herself from a futile personal battle with the child. She maintains mutual respect and a pleasant relationship with all class members by not letting them choose to side with either the teacher or the disturber. The teacher's position is not threatened, and she can truly see social growth in the class. With this feeling of satisfaction she can leave the school each day relaxed and ready to enjoy her leisure time, without anxiety.

During the past two thousand years democratic skills were not needed because, in a feudal system, decisions were made by the hierarchy or the church, and everyone knew and kept his place. But today's children are reared in a democracy that implies a right and, indeed, responsibility to express opinion for the common good. Group discussions in the classroom are essential in this democratic setting. As a group leader the teacher can get important information about the children, about individual problems, and their relationships to each other. The teacher can then guide the students in the continuous educational process.

The discussion period should not just happen as the 'need' arises but should be structured into the weekly timetable. It is essential that the pupils know that the lines of communication are open once **every** week. Even if there is little to discuss one week, the opportunity is given. It is surprising how many former problems that happened daily suddenly disappear once the discussion periods are started. Consequently, the teacher can concentrate on teaching, without so many interruptions from disturbers, or pupils with social problems in the classroom or in the yard.

When the pupils can expect their problems to be considered at the discussion time they do not go immediately to the teacher for help. They either wait patiently for a few days, or solve the problem themselves (which of course is what we are training them to do). After waiting a few days the original bad tempers have subsided and a more rational approach is possible during the presentation of the problem and discussion of the solution.

Without class discussions hostilities arise that can snowball into producing a miserable atmosphere for students and teacher alike. Group discussions provide the teacher with an opportunity to help the children understand themselves, and to change their concept of themselves and others which will eventually change their motivations from hostile to co-operative living.

The following is a suggested format for the weekly thirty minute period of class discussion. Initially, the teacher is the chairman but after the students are familiar with the process and role of the chairman (which is to conduct the proceedings and disallow rudeness, insults or word fighting), the pupils themselves can rotate this responsibility. This gives the individual pupil an opportunity to experiment with his potential leadership qualities.

At the beginning of the period there are five headings written on the blackboard or experience chart.

1. Good things of the past week.

2. Ways in which we can improve next week.

3. Personal problems.

4. Responsibilities.

5. Future plans.

As points are raised, mostly by students, they are recorded under these headings by either the teacher or the recorder, so that a summary can be quickly reviewed at the end of the session. Approximately six minutes only is recommended for discussing the topics of each heading, in order to prevent time wastage by side-tracks.

If the discussion wanders from the topic, it's the chairman's responsibility to bring it back. The teacher stresses that the pupils concentrate on the positive, expressing only supportive suggestions. When negative ideas are voiced they should be dealt with briefly, and then only in a constructive way. It is the teacher's responsibility to confront any misbehaving pupil with his mistaken goals. If this is done according to the suggestions in Chapter 4 the pupil will not feel 'put down', and the class will learn about the four goals, and possibly other children will change their own behaviour as a result of their new understanding.

Any group discussion with confrontation is as valuable for all group members as it is for the actual pupil being counselled. Many class members will have inferiority feelings. These are founded only on their own private opinions. When they hear that other pupils have similar feelings they will feel more confident about themselves. There is no doubt that class discussions are invaluable to the socialization process, to help all children feel comfortable about themselves and to aid them in the difficult process of growing up.

Group discussions serve three purposes. The first is that everybody has to learn to listen. At the present time nobody knows how the others feel. Teachers certainly are not accustomed to listen to children, and although children are forced to listen to her, they rarely know what she really feels, because of the front she usually displays.

The second function of the discussion is to help children to understand themselves and each other. To do so the teacher must be acquainted with a psychological understanding of the children, particularly of their goals. Class group discussions are centered around the goals of the child's behaviour. This eliminates fault finding, preaching, and sitting in judgment, which are all against the spirit of free discussion.

In the beginning the teacher may cite the problem of a child without mentioning a name. Soon the child will volunteer to identify himself. Children are extremely interested in such discussion and soon begin to ask personal and pertinent questions. They volunteer information about how they have tried to gain attention, show their power, get even, or give up in discouragement, although prior to the discussion they may not have realized what they were doing.

The third goal of class discussions is to stimulate each child to help the other. It is no longer the teacher with her authority and superiority who 'instructs'; the children assist each other in finding better responses to their problems. Thus, the discussion turns the class into a cohesive group. The children soon begin to feel how much they have in common. The spirit of competition becomes replaced by an atmosphere of mutual empathy and help. The weaker one, who previously was an object of scorn and contempt, now becomes a challenger for assistance. The fortunate child who succeeds socially and academically can no longer bask in the glory of his excellence, but realizes his responsibility for service to others.

In this way group discussions are more effective in changing behaviour than individual instruction. Something happens in a group discussion that has a more potent effect on behaviour than lecturing or personal help could ever achieve.

Children learn more from each other than from what the teacher says. In many cases, particularly in dealing with older and more defiant students, group discussion is the only way that they can be reached. Classroom discussions can even counteract delinquent tendencies.

The generation gap is a value gap. It can be bridged by class discussion.

Values can only be changed in a group, since every group is a value-forming agent. In this way, with the help of the rest of the students, the teacher can bring up for discussion the ideas and values of every member of the class for scrutiny and reconsideration. However, this can only be done if the teacher refrains from preaching and prevents other children from moralizing and humiliating.

For a successful discussion, the teacher, as the group leader, establishes with empathy and width of vision, a congenial group atmosphere. Only one person talks at a time and all the others learn to listen actively. No disturbance or rude interruption is accepted. The discussion stops until order is re-established. It may be advisable to appoint a secretary to take the 'minutes' and read them at the start of the next class discussion.

You, as the teacher, cannot integrate the class or win the support of the students unless you sit down with them at least once a week and talk things over. It is amazing what we can learn when we really listen to the students. We, as adults, are always inclined to over-estimate our own reactions and what happens to ourselves, and neglect seeing what we are doing to others, particularly to our pupils.

So our first step is to listen to each other; the second is to help each other to understand what each thinks, and feels. This produces an atmosphere of mutual help. The sharing of thoughts and feelings has strong therapeutic value, not only in the contents of the discussion but also in the pure freedom to talk without being 'put down' or ridiculed. Children have a need to talk, and seldom have an opportunity to discuss things that really matter to them.

Discussion is a sharing medium. The child who cannot share himself is usually a lonely child, one who is constantly on guard and afraid of being hurt. He feels threatened by the idea of giving of himself and cannot participate in a discussion on a give-and-take basis.

The introverted child will withdraw from participation in group discussion, as he withdraws from almost all participation.

You may ask "What is the value of group discussion when these individual children have such problems?" But, this is the secret – they have an opportunity to solve their problems in a non-judgemental empathetic group setting.

In a group discussion, the immediate focus is on the problem, as it affects everyone and not on the individual child. Class discussions must start as soon as the teacher becomes acquainted with her class, perhaps even on the first day of school in September. Such a discussion may concern the decorating of the classroom, planning the activities for the first week, establishing class rules, etc. Both you and the pupils may propose rules that are necessary to maintain order. They should be reasonable and understandable.

After these laws have been accepted by consensus they should be posted on a blackboard or bulletin board where all pupils can quickly refer to them.

Because these rules are logical, the pupils will want to abide by them not merely to please an authority, but because it is the proper thing to do.

"But", you may ask, "what happens if a pupil disobeys one of these rules?"

The consequences of violating a rule may be decided by the teacher immediately or by the class at the next discussion period. The important principle to be followed is that the child learns by his own experience that the infringement of order is not beneficial to him.

Here is an example: The class have agreed that playing ball near the school windows is not allowed. Billy does so and breaks a window. The class decides at the discussion period that Billy should forfeit part of his allowance over a period of time to pay for the window. In this way, Billy learns to respect property and to realize why he should not play near the windows.

It has been found that classes that have regular discussion periods have fewer incidents of vandalism, and pupils who had previously displayed delinquent behaviour became co-operative when they felt they were integrated into the group.

Prince Philip, Duke of Edinburgh, has said that segregation of all kinds is the most threatening aspect of our society. William Glasser states that integration is our only hope for relevance and involvement in education. And J. S. Mill, the nineteenth century philosopher, wrote:

"To those who have neither public nor private affections, the excitements of life are much curtailed, and in any case dwindle in value as the time approaches when all selfish interests must be terminated by death; while those who leave after them objects of personal affection, and especially those who have also cultivated a fellow-feeling with the collective interests of mankind, retain as lively an interest in life on the eve of death as in the vigour of youth and health."

chapter 11

Typical problems
and their solutions

*It seems that one purpose of education is to
turn clever children as rapidly as possible
into stupid adults.*

This sentiment has been expressed by many eminent educators. But if modern teachers were to use the two techniques of diagnosing the four goals and integrating the class, we would soon reverse the above statement, and turn most children into co-operative adults.

Here are some examples of typical misbehaviour by children in the elementary school. See if you can guess the child's mistaken goal (1) Attention (2) Power (3) Revenge (4) Display of inadequacy. Remember that the unconscious goal is often the unadmitted goal. When diagnosing the child's immediate mistaken goal it is advisable to consider the following:

1. What did the description of the behaviour really say about the child's purpose?

2. What was the teacher's feeling response to the inappropriate behavior?

3. What did the teacher do that possibly reinforced the mistaken goal?

4. What was the child's next move?

> Kathy has dropped her pencil deliberately for the fifth time this morning. This has happened many times in the past few weeks. The teacher feels annoyed. She has repeatedly reminded Kathy to be more careful and has often talked and scolded her about the disturbances. Now the teacher feels that Kathy occupies too much of her teaching time.

The mistaken goal is Goal 1 (Attention). After the teacher has confirmed her suspicion by confrontation, and by seeing the recognition reflex, she can then apply the corrective procedure. She will ignore the pencil dropping at this time but will talk to Kathy later. She will compliment Kathy on her co-operative behaviour whenever possible; show an interest in her, but never at the time when Kathy demands or expects it, and gradually show her that she is accepted and does belong to the class group. Then there will be no need for Kathy to drop her pencil for recognition.

> Johnny refuses to finish his arithmetic and is scribbling on his paper. Johnny is also sullen and defiant. After the principal had punished him, he threw a brick through the classroom window. When he plays ball with the other boys and his team is losing he always moans and calls the opposing team cheaters. The teacher wishes Johnny were not in her class. She feels hurt and outraged by his behaviour. She even dislikes him and often says, "How can he be so mean?"

You've guessed it. The mistaken goal is Goal 3 (Revenge). After confronting Johnny with the goals, and establishing this fact, she begins her plan of action. Even though she feels like telling him how hurt she is she avoids the slightest indication. She decides not to punish or shout at him again. She does unexpected things that please and surprise him. She encourages the group to like and support him. At the class discussion she asks for a volunteer to be his helpful buddy and friend. Within a short time she finds that he asks for help with his arithmetic and no longer scribbles on his paper. He now puts forth a real effort in the arithmetic lesson.

Bob has just thrown a spitball across the room. The teacher has asked him to write an assignment about wolves but he is stubborn and, as usual, does the opposite to instructions. He is in a particularly bad temper today, has argued constantly with his classmates and done no work in any lesson. The teacher feels defeated and begins to think, "He can't do this to me". At the moment the spitball whizzes past her ear she feels that her leadership is threatened. She yells, "Bob, you can't get away with this."

No doubt you discovered the goal at the beginning. Bob is a typical 'power drunk' child in Goal 2. When the teacher diagnoses his goal she will admit defeat, inwardly or openly, or both. She will recognize Bob's power and give him opportunities to use it constructively. At all costs she will avoid a power struggle with him and extricate herself from any conflict. She will show respect for Bob—even for the fact that he seems to have more power in the classroom than she has. She will not fight with him as he wants her to do—that would mean giving in to his provocation. By remaining kind and firm, she can lead him to find his place through better alternatives.

Joan has withdrawn and continues to stare blankly out of the window. She feels hopeless and acts "stupid". She appears to have an inferiority complex and rarely participates but always gives up. She seems to be saying subconsciously, "Leave me alone, you can't do anything with me". As Joan sits slumped at her desk, the teacher passes by and ignores the situation. The teacher really feels helpless and throws up her hands thinking "I don't know what to do with you; I give up."

After confirming the guess of Goal 4 (Display of inadequacy) the teacher begins a strenuous encouragement programme. She makes Joan feel worthwhile when she tries and encourages her, particularly when she makes mistakes. The teacher uses a constructive approach and enlists the class co-operation with pupil helpers. The aim of the teacher is to show Joan that she has faith in her abilities to cope and meet the needs of the situation. Often the members of the class can exert a strong encouraging influence, by showing their pleasure when the child shows an improvement, however slight it may be.

chapter 12

Examples that stopped the tears

When we deal with a child, even the most difficult one, we must have faith in him or her. Pessimism gains nothing; optimism is the only way to improve and change behaviour in others.

This book is written in an informal way in order that it may help not only the individual dedicated to the career of teaching in schools but also the person who thinks of teaching as a temporary job, e.g. Brownie and Cub leaders, Sunday school teachers, camp counsellors etc. The following examples are the personal experiences of one of the authors with elementary school children:

Johnny, aged 11, often displayed Goal 2 (Power) and Goal 3 (Revenge) behaviour. He was repeatedly late after recess. One day I explained to the class that immediately after recess we would all be making a film strip. We were all very excited about this and had planned the sequence of the story of Theseus and the Minotaur, with printing and drawings.

The children returned after recess and I gave them detailed instructions regarding size and dimensions. Johnny appeared after these instructions were given. He saw that the class were working. After sitting down at his seat he said, "Can I do what they are doing?" I said, "Yes, you may." He looked at the work that the other children were doing, but they did not explain to him the importance of dimensions. He spent a full half hour busily drawing and printing. At the end of the lesson, the pupils were displaying their work for evaluation. When Johnny held up his work a classmate said, "We can't use that for our filmstrip because it is the wrong dimensions for the camera." Johnny said, "Nobody told me what the dimensions were. Another classmate said, "Teacher told us, right after recess, and you weren't here."

Johnny was dreadfully upset. His was the only piece of work that was not photographed.

Tearfully, he left the classroom, taking his work home with him. After that day he was never late from recess again.

The logical consequence taught him far more effectively than any punishment. He learned without receiving special attention from the teacher or fighting in a power struggle. And the result of this learning was a permanent change in behaviour.

The following is an example of a nine year old boy with severe spelling difficulties (and, as usual with spelling problems, he had little respect for order). Tim was withdrawn, deeply discouraged, in Goal 4 and showing continuous displays of inadequacy. He would even say, "Don't mark my work because I know it is all wrong."

A class project was started to improve the general standards of spelling, and the pupils worked in five separate groups. The word lists were compiled on Mondays, studied during the week in various ways, then tested on Fridays.

During a weekly discussion period, Tim's group complained that he was getting so many words incorrect that he was spoiling their improvement chart. They even wanted to evict him from their group. I asked them what they had done to help Tim. They replied "Nothing". I then said, "What could you do to help him?" They suggested that some of them could help him after classes in the afternoons. I asked Tim if he would like them to help him at this time. He appeared delighted. His group set up a schedule for the four days. Each afternoon a different volunteer played spelling games with him for ten minutes. On the following Friday he got all his words right. He was completely surprised and overjoyed. His group enthusiastically congratulated him. This procedure was repeated for three more weeks with a decreasing number of help periods until finally he managed to study his word list himself with satisfactory results.

The next example is a situation that was first mentioned at the class discussion. It was during the winter time and one pupil made the following statement: "Our room looks a mess because there are always so many coats, hats and mitts lying on the floor at the back of the room even though there's lots of coat hangers."

Another child said, "If anything is on the floor it should either be put in the garbage can or take it to the 'lost and found' box." Another child suggested the idea that any clothing on the floor should automatically go to the 'lost and found'. It was agreed by consensus that this should immediately take effect. (concensus means a unanimous agreement, **not** a majority vote). The next morning there were about fifteen coats and hats lying on the floor. I said nothing but one of the children picked up an armful of clothes and asked his friend to help him. They both struggled to the box with all this clothing.

At recess there were fifteen children rumaging through the 'lost and found' box for clothing. They missed most of their playtime. On the next day there were seven coats on the floor and the following morning there were only three. Within a week we had eliminated the whole problem of clothing on the floor. The suggestion had come from the group and the problem was solved by the group without any suggestion from me. This was truly group awareness in action.

At a later discussion period a pupil raised the point that Jack and Gary were spoiling their gymnastics lesson. I asked Jack and Gary if this were true. They admitted it. After considerable discussion it was suggested by a class member that, at the beginning of the gymnastics lesson, Jack and Gary would be allowed to demonstrate certain movements and somersaults of their choice, and the class would follow, and repeat these activities. This was agreed by consensus and the class co-operated in the next gymnastic lesson. After that there were no more disturbances from Gary or Jack.

Here are some more typical problems and their solutions. Try to solve the problem before you read the answer.

Look for the clues: the description of the child's behaviour; the actions of the teacher; and the words used to express the teacher's feelings Annoyance indicates goal 1, defeat—

Goal 2; outrage—Goal 3; and helplessness—Goal 4. After referring to the Goals Chart in Chapter 4, choose the corrective procedures the teacher might use.

PROBLEM ONE

David is sitting, occasionally glancing around, and doing his mathematics as slowly as possible. He writes three numerals and rubs out two. He tries to write them better. Finally, after fifteen minutes he is satisfied so gives his attention to the second simple question. Meanwhile the teacher has been moving about the room helping others and reminding David to "hurry up". The teacher keeps wondering how she is going to make David work faster.

David is discouraged, has a poor self image and is probably over ambitious. The teacher has **fallen** for David's mistaken goal (Goal 1) of attention getting by constantly reminding him to hurry. The teacher has taken his responsibility for herself and has made David's problem her problem. He feels that he has a place in the class only when his work is perfect. He feels worthwhile only when he is on top. After confronting him with the four goals, and establishing he is in fact in Goal 1, the teacher should do the following things to help David. She will encourage him not to be afraid to make mistakes, give him assurance that he is accepted as he is. Assure him that he does not have to be perfect to be worthwhile. She will give him lots of attention but only at times when he does not demand or expect it. She helps him with work that he truly does not understand. She will not remind him in class to hurry but help him to make goals for himself regarding his assignments and then leave him alone to complete them.

PROBLEM TWO

Mary puts up her hand and tells the teacher she doesn't know what to do. The exasperated teacher looks at Mary and asks if she was listening to the instructions. The teacher is annoyed at Mary and her voice indicates it. Mary has made a habit of not knowing what to do, and the teacher often reminds her of this in front of the class.

Mary is in Goal 1 – a destructive-attention getter, and the teacher is reinforcing Mary's mistaken goal. The clue to the child's misbehaviour as being in Goal 1 is the teacher's reaction - her annoyance. Instead of encouraging Mary to be responsible for herself, she further discourages Mary by embarrassing her. And Mary feels obliged to live **down** to the teacher's expectations. After confronting Mary with the four goals to confirm that Mary is bidding unduly for attention the teacher can decide that she will no longer show annoyance. She will encourage Mary to listen, but not repeat the instructions. If Mary does not know what to do, she will be unable to finish the assignment in the required time. The logical consequence would be to finish in her own time after school. She would then learn to listen in future.

PROBLEM THREE
Susan is playing with the doll's house in the kindergarten. Jane has been waiting patiently for her turn. The teacher suggests that Jane have a turn. Susan throws down the doll, kicks the doll house and then kicks the teacher. The teacher wonders why Susan is so mean.

The clue to the mistaken goal on which Susan is operating is the teacher's reaction. The teacher thought, "How mean can Susan be?" Susan's mistaken goal is Goal 3. Her misbehaviour of throwing the doll, kicking the doll's house and the teacher is an active-destructive way of seeking her place. And we must realize that all behaviours, whether good or bad, of children under 10 are directed toward the adult in order to gain significance. After Susan has calmed down the teacher should confront her with the four goals to discover if it really is Goal 3. She will then encourage Susan to feel that she is liked, perhaps by enlisting a volunteer buddy from the class. She will praise Susan when her behaviour is acceptable and be silent when it is not. She will constantly try to give Susan the feeling of belonging and sharing with the other children. When the teacher believes that Susan can behave in a socially acceptable manner it is likely that she will respond to that trust.

PROBLEM FOUR
Betty is very quiet in the classroom and never participates in the discussion periods. She often 'forgets' to

hand in assignments and when given a test rarely gets past the first question. On the day that a field trip was planned for the class she stayed at home, although she was not ill. The teacher has tried many times to interest Betty, but has never seen enthusiasm for anything. The teacher doesn't know what to do with her.

Betty is passive and self-defeated. She wants to be left alone and acts as if she is inferior and incapable. Since the teacher feels helpless, and Betty's social interest is so poorly developed that she does not even want to go on a field trip, we might guess that her mistaken goal is Goal 4. By confrontation the teacher could confirm this. Betty's deep discouragement is crying out for reassurance. At the weekly class discussion the teacher will give Betty opportunities to contribute, and encourage the other children to include Betty in their activities. As Betty's confidence in her social relationships grows she will feel more capable to tackle her work. When she feels that she really belongs, she will likely 'remember' to hand in the assignments.

PROBLEM FIVE
Paul constantly argues with the teacher. In every science or history lesson he interrupts, saying that the teacher is wrong. When he is asked to read his text book he deliberately tells jokes to the other students to distract them. Most of the teacher's lessons are spoiled by Paul. Whatever the teacher asks him to do, he does the opposite. The teacher feels exasperated and often thinks "Who is running this class, he or I"?

Paul is a typical power-drunk boy who feels he has to control and challenge leadership in order to belong. By arguing, distracting and showing defiance, he opposes the teacher. The teacher feels threatened in her role and is continually in a power conflict with the Goal 2 boy. After confronting Paul with the goals to find out if her guess is right, she will help Paul by giving him important and 'powerful' things to do in the class, that are acceptable and in line with the progress of the class. She will not compete with him, but enlist his cooperation as an ally. When he argues, she will extricate herself from the conflict by remaining calm and saying nothing.

Examples/95

Or publicly give him credit for disturbing the class by telling him unemotionally "You have a point" By the teacher showing respect for Paul he will learn that he does not have to challenge in order to be part of the class. At the weekly class discussion period Paul can interact with his classmates less aggressively and gradually contribute positively.

PROBLEM SIX
Jim walks into the history class, looks around, sits down and starts to play with his pen. As the lesson proceeds it is obvious to the teacher that Jim is taking no part in the lesson. He spends most of his time gazing out of the window. After the assignment is given the teacher walks around and notices that Jim has made no attempt to even start the assignment. The teacher tells Jim he will have to come back after school if he doesn't finish the assignment in class. Jim shrugs his shoulders and tells her that every other teacher wants him to stay as well. The teacher feels helpless and doesn't know what to do.

Jim's behaviour of being an observer, rather than a participator in the class is a symptom of his feelings of inadequacy. The teacher's reaction of feeling helpless indicates that she has fallen for his mistaken goal (Goal 4). Obviously threat of punishment has not changed Jim's direction. He has given up, does not even try, and has become so discouraged that he inhibits his own ability to learn. After confronting Jim with his mistaken goals to confirm the suspicion of Goal 4 (Display of inadequacy) the teacher embarks on an encouragement programme. Perhaps she can influence other teachers who are also having trouble with Jim. If the work assignments are within Jim's capabilities she may get another student to sit with him. She can decide to mark only his correct responses, and ignore the mistakes, in order to help him feel that he is making some progress. She can tell the class sincerely that Jim, who has got four correct answers out of fifty has improved 100%, because in the last lesson he only got two right.

In these examples we learn that the class discussion period can be vitally important to the healthy growth of the class as a group, and an essential encouragement process for misbehaving discouraged pupils. As the teacher learns to talk less, act more and respect students as individuals with enormous potential, she can then teach in a co-operative atmosphere where students are willing to learn and discipline problems are minimal. When the pressure of conflict is relaxed the teacher's own potential can then be released and the creativity of the students can be expressed. If learning and intelligence are creative then we must provide the optimum environment for this growth in our classrooms.

As you apply the principles that are explained in this book you will be a happier, healthier and more relaxed teacher. Children's tears and your tears will be a bad memory of the past. You will find joy in your profession by sharing the ecstasy of life experiences with children who are eager to discover, explore, and share their new found feelings with you ... their teacher, leader and friend.

DISCIPLINE
WITHOUT
TEARS
WORKBOOK

David Kehoe

Author's note

Every effort has been made to keep the tone of this workbook in tune with the informal spirit of the text, <u>Discipline Without Tears</u>. This book has been designed as an aid to learning and a check (not test) of <u>your</u> understanding of the text. Three kinds of questions appear randomly distributed throughout each chapter review: multiple choice, modified true/false, and recall, i.e., fill in the blanks. The style of questioning is intended to provide both interest and a challenge while you work through the exercises.

Some of the questions may seem moot; however, if you disagree with any of the answers given in the "Answers to Exercises" section, remember that for the purpose of this workbook the text <u>Discipline Without Tears</u> is the ultimate source. In fact, it is hoped that the questions presented will stimulate some animated discussions.

I would like to express my thanks to Mrs. Pearl Cassel for not only giving me the opportunity to work on this project, but also for her continual encouragement and helpful suggestions.

chapter 1
What kind of teacher are you?

1. An autocratic boss usually suffers from feelings of _____.
    (a) superiority
    (b) inadequacy
    (c) arrogance
    (d) power

2. The efforts of a classroom dictator invariably lead to _____.
    (a) success
    (b) fear
    (c) defeat
    (d) rejection

3. Today's children reject the tyrant because they are aware of _____.
    (a) the power they possess
    (b) the weakness of the tyrant
    (c) the implications of a democratic society
    (d) the prevailing democratic atmosphere

4. The autocratic teacher with problem children in the classroom _____.
    (a) may be the major cause
    (b) has little effect on the development
    (c) has no responsibility for the cause
    (d) has little knowledge

5. The fact that most problem teenagers are living in _____ demonstrates that these teenagers have not developed a sense of responsibility toward their fellow man.
    (a) a state of euphoria

(b) a state of democratic ideals
(c) a state of hyperactivity
(d) a state of infantile selfishness

6.   The autocratic teacher tends to (generate/
retard) problem behavior in children.

7.   A rigidly structured class conducted by (an
autocratic/a democratic) teacher breeds
(confidence/arrogance) in what one would generally consider a good child.

8.   "Bad" children can be made worse by
(ignoring/punishing) or (discouraging/chastising)
them.

9.   (Equally as/less) harmful to the child
(than/as) the autocratic teacher is the too permissive one.

10.   An autocratically dominated classroom (does
have/does not have much of) an effect on the
social and emotional growth of a mentally healthy
child.

11.   A good teacher provides an abundance of visual aids, opportunities for independent learning, and a free choice of topics to be studied
in a _____ situation.

12.   Permissive teachers, like autocratic teachers, tend to produce _____ children
by their methods.

13.   To choose between a _____ teacher and a(n) _____ teacher is not to
have a choice between the lesser of two evils
because _____ have essentially abdicated their _____.

14.   In addition to helping the child's social
and emotional growth, a teacher is responsible
for teaching the child to _____,
_____, and _____ in order
that he will be able to cope with many of life's
situations.

15.   The alternative to the autocratic boss or
the laissez-faire anarchist is a good
_____ leader.

16. The essential difference between the autocratic teacher and the democratic leader is that
the first _____ pressure from
_____ while the democratic leader
produces the _____ pressure from
_____.

17. In the list below underline those qualities or characteristics you would expect to
find in a democratic leader.
    (a) friendly voice
    (b) pressure
    (c) influence
    (d) demands cooperation
    (e) criticism
    (f) stimulation
    (g) winning cooperation
    (h) punishing
    (i) acknowledgment of achievement
    (j) shares responsibility

chapter 2
A rewarding alternative

1. Discipline and control must be present in
the classroom if _____.
    (a) you want to avoid disruptive behavior
    (b) you are a good teacher
    (c) effective learning is to take place
    (d) you want a quiet atmosphere

2. We can overcome (most/all) discipline problems if we accept a philosophy based on principles of freedom and responsibility.

3. Teachers must learn to become a match for
their students without being _____ or _____.
(Pick the two most appropriate words.)
    (a) punitive
    (b) democratic
    (c) a conformist
    (d) too firm
    (e) permissive

4. Democracy is more than a political ideal;
it is a way of life in which _____
must govern freedom.

5. It is what you learn that allows you _____.
    (a) to be less disciplined
    (b) to keep out of trouble
    (c) to be free

6. _____ is the seed from which freedom grows.
    (a) Learning
    (b) Discipline
    (c) Money
    (d) Democracy

7. If an individual develops the skills of cooperation, a willingness to learn, and making appropriate decisions, he will most likely develop the ability to use _____.

8. The inability to use _____ to make appropriate decisions can badly affect personal relationships.
    (a) our personality
    (b) problem-solving techniques
    (c) our influence
    (d) our learned social behavior

9. Without a wide variety of skills we (can/cannot) be forced into a virtually choiceless environment.

10. Assumed _____ without skills or _____ makes one truly dependent on those with the appropriate skills.

11. A democratic teacher (has/does not have) a greater influence on pupils than an autocratic teacher has.

12. A democratic leader can best teach the philosophy of freedom by _____.
    (a) being on constant guard against encroachments of subversive groups
    (b) by being kind and permissive
    (c) by extending the idea of her philosophy to other teachers
    (d) by assuming the role of responsible guide

13. A teacher's freedom helps her students learn best how to _____.

14. Good mental health in the classroom depends upon which six of the following realizations? (Underline them.)
    (a) You must guard your own mental health.
    (b) You have a high I.Q. and can expect to be hurt because of the supersensitivity this gives you.
    (c) You do a good job because that is what you are paid to do.
    (d) You like teaching children.
    (e) You enjoy some form of recreation.

(f) You must accept and understand your-
    self.
(g) You accept children as being part of
    the job.
(h) You accept challenges with confidence.
(i) You will be a better teacher if you
    dedicate yourself exclusively to your
    job.
(j) You work for a sense of accomplishment.

15. Quiet action in dealing with a problem is
always more effective than _____.
    (a) repeating directions
    (b) words
    (c) criticizing
    (d) giving sound advice

16. A classroom situation (can/cannot) be both
free and yet controlled.

17. A teacher's attitude to freedom is crucial
because _____.
    (a) he has a responsibility to society
    (b) he must conduct a good program
    (c) he knows an autocratic teacher is a bad
        teacher
    (d) his influence is long lasting

chapter 3
How does a child grow?

1. According to Dr. Dreikurs, the only experience that can truly promote a child's growth and
development is _____.
   (a) avoidance of mistake-centered situa-
       tions
   (b) firm self-discipline
   (c) the experience of utilizing one's own
       strengths
   (d) living in a democratic society

2. In order to help a child develop to the
fullest of his potential, we (should/should not)
be concerned with the generalized sequential
progression of social and emotional growth.

3. By anticipating certain behavior and reactions from children teachers most likely promote those reactions because _____.
   (a) children have a sense of freedom
   (b) children quickly learn the conse-
       quences of their actions
   (c) children behave as their teachers tell
       them
   (d) children often behave in line with
       adults' expectations

4. According to Dreikurs and Cassel, the three
phases of childhood are _____, _____, and _____.
   (a) prenatal environment
   (b) preschool family life
   (c) elementary school days
   (d) peer group influences
   (e) adolescence

5. At which phase of childhood mentioned in Question 4 above is a child's life style formed? _____

6. _____ action of a child is an attempt to find his place in the group.

7. In which of the following is the child weakest? _____
    (a) input
    (b) observation
    (c) interpretation
    (d) assimilation
    (e) output

8. In order to maintain good mental health an individual must _____ and _____.

9. At which age can a child begin to manipulate his parents? _____
    (a) 0-1 (b) 1-2 (c) 2-3 (d) 3-4

10. Organ inferiority (is/is not) an active response of heredity endowment.

11. With a physically handicapped individual _____ exerts a stronger force on his behavior than does his handicap.

12. A physically healthy child with a behavior problem (may/may not) over-compensate.

13. It (is/is not) essential for a teacher to know a child's I.Q. score in order to best teach that child.

14. Teachers should expect _____ children to be responsible human beings.

15. The major effort to help children (should/ should not) be made at the elementary school level (because/although) they (can/cannot) be helped at the secondary school level.

16. Any child who has a sequence of bad teachers who continually tell him he is a failure _____.
    (a) is a hopeless case

(b) can be helped
(c) is lost forever
(d) can never gain self-respect

17. A teacher's _____ and
_____ are very important because of
the strong influence of his example.

review of chapters 1-3

1. The _____ teacher tends to generate problem behavior in children.

2. A "bad" child can be made worse by _____ or _____ him.

3. Which two kinds of teachers cause equal harm in the classroom?
     (a) autocratic
     (b) liberal
     (c) democratic
     (d) permissive

4. Which kinds of teachers have a strong effect on the emotional and social growth of mentally healthy children?
     (a) autocratic
     (b) liberal
     (c) democratic
     (d) permissive

5. Complete the following analogy: Autocrat is to external pressure as democratic is to _____.

6. Democracy succeeds only if freedom is accompanied by _____.

7. The degree and quality of freedom enjoyed by any individual are determined primarily by the degree and quality of _____.

8. Our personal relationships are affected by our ability to use _____ techniques.

9. That you accept and understand yourself is a sign of good _____.

10. The experience of utilizing one's own strengths will promote a child's _____ and _____ much more effectively than any knowledge of a sequential progression of social and emotional growth.

11. A child's life style is most likely formed during the _____ period.

12. To be a successful human being one's _____ is more important than one's ability.

13. To most effectively change behavior we must change the _____.

14. Children most likely misbehave because they are operating on a system of _____.

15. We need to ask all four "Could it be . . ." questions because a child may have _____.

chapter 4
Understanding the modern child

1. When we are confronted with a problem child we should not be discouraged because children have _____ for social interest.

2. The teacher (is/is not) mostly to blame if a child is discouraged and becomes a problem because other adults with whom the child comes in contact have (little effect/as much an effect) on moulding his attitudes.

3. In order to more effectively change behavior you must ____.
    (a) increase classroom standards
    (b) increase external incentives
    (c) be less concerned with motivation in the classroom
    (d) find ways to utilize intrinsic motivation

4. A child misbehaves to gain social acceptance because he is operating on a system of _____.

5. We should avoid criticizing a misbehaving child because ____.
    (a) a hostile child does not learn new behavior adjustments
    (b) he is only trying to find his place
    (c) a hostile child is extrinsically motivated
    (d) he is only trying to gain your attention

6. According to Dreikurs and Cassel, what is the maximum age at which we can most effectively help a child by modifying his motivation? _____

7. Once we have modified a child's behavior to what we expect we (can/cannot) assume that we have used an effective method of correction.

8. We should not be surprised at the number of problem children in our more affluent urban way of life because _____.
   (a) today's children are aware of their role in the family unit
   (b) today's children are more inept at performing tasks than children of a generation ago
   (c) today's children find few ways to be useful and contribute to the family's welfare
   (d) today's children are aware of the implications of a democratic society

9. The behavior of a problem child will become more constructive if we modify the (behavior/motivation).

10. When teachers notice a child switching from one kind of behavior to another, they should be aware that this may signify a _____ of the problem.
   (a) lessening
   (b) deepening
   (c) both of the above
   (d) either (a) or (b)
   (e) none of the above

11. To recognize the goal a misbehaving child is using the teacher should _____.
   (a) try to reason with the child
   (b) understand the purpose of his behavior
   (c) be understanding and wait quietly until the tantrum has finished

12. The most accurate clue to discovering the child's goal is _____.
   (a) the child's answer to the question, "Could it be that . . .?"

(b) the form his behavior takes
(c) to be aware of the four goals of chil-
    dren's misbehavior
(d) your immediate response to his be-
    havior

13. A child (can/cannot) have more than one
goal operating at the same time, and it is for
this reason that all four of the "Could it
be . . ." questions (should/need not) be asked.

chapter 5
Competition

1. Competition (is/is not) good for young children because it (helps/does not help) them draw closer together in an atmosphere of comradeship and team spirit.

2. It (is/is not) true that because competition for marks, grades, treats, or prizes is a division factor in a classroom we should not give achievement tests to children under ten.

3. Competition:
    (a) is the only fair way in a democratic society to select people for certain tasks.
    (b) is a rewarding experience for only a few individuals.
    (c) is a rewarding experience for most individuals.
    (d) is a good method of motivating learning.

4. A (competitive/noncompetitive) person can function better as a human being in a competitive society.

5. Which of the following characteristics would you expect to see in a person trained in a noncompetitive situation?
    (a) He is concerned with others as friends.
    (b) He is not hung up on feelings of superiority.
    (c) He functions well when he wins.
    (d) He wastes energy blaming others.
    (e) He respects himself.

(f) He finds it difficult to adjust to a life of equality.
(g) He has the courage to be imperfect.
(h) He finds it relatively easy to work as part of a team.
(i) He has a good sense of fellowship.

6. Many teenagers suffer from infantile self-ishness because ____.
    (a) most training at all levels is com-petitive
    (b) children are naturally selfish
    (c) they have not grown up
    (d) their parents have overindulged them

7. Children (can/cannot) help other children to adjust.

8. A spirit of cooperation and helpfulness can best be achieved if the teacher uses a _____ approach with students.

9. A child, like an adult, is a _____.

chapter 6
Encouragement

1. As teachers we tend to avoid helping those children who need encouragement most because _____.
    - (a) our reaction to them makes them worse
    - (b) only some children deserve our attention
    - (c) we cannot help them
    - (d) they usually behave in a distasteful manner

2. In order to increase a child's self-confidence we concomitantly strengthen his _____.

3. Too many adults as well as children waste their potential _____.
    - (a) by not trying hard enough
    - (b) by trying to be perfect
    - (c) by not accepting the standards of their peers
    - (d) by refusing to adequately tax their minds

4. Which of the following is the most important aspect of encouragement? _____
    - (a) What one does.
    - (b) What one says.
    - (c) How one does it.

5. A mentally healthy child (can/cannot) become discouraged and participate in antisocial behavior.

6. Here are some statements based on the twenty points to encourage every student. Make each statement true by removing the appropriate word.

      (a) Work for (improvement/perfection).
      (b) One's (efforts/results) are more signif-
          icant than one's (efforts/results).
      (c) Build on (strengths/weaknesses).
      (d) The best measure of one's (worth/skill)
          is success.
      (e) Praise is not the same as (encouragement/
          discouragement).

7. Encouragement is needed by _____ children.
      (a) most   (b) few   (c) all   (d) some

8. Praise may give the child the impression that the opinion of others is a measure of his _____ and will probably carry over into adulthood.

9. Praise can be a negative thing: It may even counter what we are trying to do and be very _____ for a child.

10. In order to successfully encourage a child we must be alert to _____.
      (a) his response to praise
      (b) his degree of competitiveness
      (c) his emotional growth
      (d) his training and background

11. Inappropriate praise tends to make the individual too _____.

12. Can you distinguish the crucial difference between praise and encouragement? Underline only those statements below which illustrate encouragement.
      (a) You're wonderful to do this.
      (b) We appreciate all the help you have
          given.
      (c) I'm glad you enjoyed doing that paint-
          ing.
      (d) My, but you're a pretty little girl.
      (e) You've made a great deal of improvement
          in your writing.

13. As important as what you say to encourage
a child is the way you say it. "We like you,
but we don't like what you do" may be an encouraging thing to say, but it can discourage a
child if said in the wrong _____.

14. What remarks might you make to a child to
encourage him? See if you can match the appropriate remarks from Column A with the statements
in Column B. There are more comments than you
will need.

A	B

(a) Let's try and   (a) Progress is
    work this out to-   something we
    gether.   should expect
(b) Okay, let's see   from all chil-
    what we can   dren.
    learn from this   (b) It is important
    mistake.   to distinguish
(c) Try this: I know   between the
    you can do it,   child and his
    but if you need   behavior.
    my help ask me.   (c) It is important
(d) I like you, but   to involve chil-
    I don't like what   dren in group
    you did.   projects.
(e) Keep trying;   (d) Teachers should
    don't give up.   express confi-
(f) I am glad to see   dence in a
    the improvement   child's ability
    in your writing.   to resolve his
(g) You little jerk,   own conflicts.
    smarten up.   (e) We should avoid
                             embarrassing
                             children.

15. A good way to see that a child does not
feel a sense of fulfillment or self-acceptance
or hold a belief that he can achieve is to make
sure that he meets with little _____.

16. _____ and _____
nourish aggression, conflict, and deviant behavior.

review of chapters 4-6

1. Because children have an innate capacity
for social interest we should not be
_____ when confronted with a problem
child.

2. By utilizing intrinsic motivation we can
most effectively _____ of a problem
child.

3. A child generally _____ because
he is operating on a system of _____.

4. The four goals of misbehavior identified
by Dr. Dreikurs are: _____,
_____, _____, and
_____.

5. The teacher's emotional response to a
child's behavior is the most accurate clue to
discovering the child's _____.

6. A _____ person can survive better in our society because he is not concerned
with what others are doing.

7. One of the most discouraging methods of
motivating learning is _____, which
only a few children find a rewarding experience.

8. A spirit of cooperation and helpfulness
can best be fostered by a _____ approach with students.

9.   Democratic teaching usually produces
_____ results, while competitive
training usually produces only _____
results.

10.   Like all of us, children are _____,
not miniature or incomplete adults, and as such
deserve the same respect as any other.

11.   Teachers tend to _____ helping
discouraged youngsters who behave in a distaste-
ful manner.

12.   As teachers we need to encourage
_____ children.

13.   _____ can be a harmful thing because it may give a child the impression that
what others think of him is a measure of his
personal worth.

14.   As important as _____ you say
to a child is the _____ you say it.

15.   You must structure your teaching to accommodate the child's ability because it is essential that a child meet with a great deal of
_____ in order to feel a sense of
fulfillment and self-acceptance.

chapter 7
Logical consequences,
not punishment

1. In a democratic setting _____ is ineffective.

2. Punishment yields only _____ results.
   (a) lasting
   (b) desirable
   (c) temporary
   (d) effective

3. A system of reward and punishment is (essential/detrimental) to the rearing of children.

4. Permissiveness (is/is not) the alternative to abandoning a system of reward and punishment.

5. A permissive atmosphere breeds _____.
   (a) mutual equality and respect
   (b) anarchy and chaos
   (c) order and discipline
   (d) a relaxed atmosphere

6. Bribery is a form of _____ which is what we are trying to avoid.

7. Children trained in an atmosphere of (competition/cooperation) are more likely to feel worthwhile and accepted.

8. In order to accept the philosophy that children can be trained without the use of threat and punishment you must first accept the idea that _____.
   (a) punishment is effective but evil

      (b) men are basically competitive and we
          must change this
      (c) all men are created equal
      (d) man is basically cooperative

9. If a child continually and purposely falls off a chair and hurts himself, this is a (natural/logical) consequence; but if the teacher removes the chair so that he cannot use it, this is a (natural/logical) consequence.

10. You recall that the four mistaken goals of behavior (Chart 2) are attention, power, revenge, and inadequacy. Each of these goals calls for an effective correction procedure. Tell which of the procedures you would use [(a) logical consequences, (b) natural consequences, (c) neither] to help correct the misbehavior symptomatic of each goal below.

      Goal 1   a, b, c
      Goal 2   a, b, c
      Goal 3   a, b, c
      Goal 4   a, b, c

11. Can you tell the difference between logical consequences and punishment? Underline only the phrases below that characterize logical consequences:

      (a) inevitably involves moral judgment
      (b) distinguishes between deed and doer
      (c) implies that the child has little or
          no value
      (d) adult permits no choice
      (e) adult tries to be objective
      (f) respects the child
      (g) voice is loud and angry
      (h) concerned with what will happen now

12. The use of logical consequences rather than punishment allows the _____ to make a decision.

13. Logical consequences can be turned into futile punishment if _____.

      (a) the pupils see the teacher is weak
      (b) the teacher becomes upset and personally involved

(c) the pupils do not immediately respond
(d) the teacher does not immediately respond

14. _____ must be a logical or natural outcome of a series of events.

chapter 8

Conflict solving and how to deal with tyrants

1. In any relationship of mutual respect between pupil and teacher, the teacher must not only be kind but also _____.

2. A child needs a good teacher or other adult guide because _____.
    (a) he is a good observer
    (b) he is a poor interpreter
    (c) he is exposed to more mass media
    (d) he is a dignified human being

3. Which of the following are useful conflict solving techniques:
    (a) fighting with the child
    (b) giving in to the child
    (c) waiting until a tantrum is over
    (d) a well structured logical argument
    (e) firmly removing the child from the conflict situation

4. Conflicts are _____ because of differences of opinions, interests, and goals.

5. Of the different types of problem children which type is the most difficult for teachers to cope with? _____

6. If a teacher understands the four goals of misbehavior, she will be better equipped to _____ her class.
    (a) dominate
    (b) coerce
    (c) influence
    (d) tolerate

7. A prerequisite to solving conflict situations between two people is _____.

8. In what age group are the goals of misbehavior easiest to define? _____

9. A conflict situation cannot be resolved as long as both parties involved _____ to fight.

10. In order that all pupils may share in the decision-making process, the teacher should provide opportunities for group discussions. To be most effective these discussions should be _____.
           (a) regularly scheduled
           (b) introduced as each new problem arises
           (c) conducted occasionally
           (d) avoided if possible

11. In order to succeed in solving any conflict we must first change (our own/our opponent's) attitude.

12. We can best live with tyrants if we _____.
           (a) give in
           (b) show we are as strong as they are
           (c) show we respect them as human beings
           (d) completely ignore them

chapter 9
Is your class a group?

1. We should spend more time ____.
   - (a) struggling with untrained children
   - (b) training children to socialize in group life
   - (c) making children a mirror of our personality
   - (d) trying to become a member of a group

2. Teachers often fail to recognize children's strengths and capacities because of a deep and unrecognized _____.

3. To the group leader the size of the class, within reasonable limits, (is/is not) significant.

4. Homogeneity in age and abilities (is/is not) essential for the successful operation of group dynamics.

5. It is essential to integrate groups of children on a regular basis in order to maintain group (cohesiveness/cooperation).

6. What is a good test for teachers to use to help them understand and integrate subgroups?

_____

7. The test (see No. 6 above) is twofold; it is _____ as well as a basis for changes in relationships.

8. The key characteristic of such a test is ____.
   - (a) that it must have no spelling errors

    (b) that it must not ask for personal
         opinions
    (c) that any critical answers must not name
         specific people
    (d) that it must be meaningful and within
         the realm of reality

9. In a group project each individual will
most likely contribute more with the least friction if _____.
    (a) the members are highly intelligent
    (b) the members are all from the same class
    (c) the members are compatible
    (d) the teacher has good control of the
         class

10. Isolates should be encouraged to join extroverted groups so they may have an opportunity
to develop _____ skill.

11. In order to help an isolate the teacher
should _____.
    (a) sensibly avoid any interference
    (b) discuss with him the value of social
         intercourse
    (c) deliberately steer him to a group
    (d) make groups accept him into their
         games

12. A teacher should repeat the sociometric
test procedures several times throughout the
year because group relationships _____.

review of chapters 7-9

1. As a method of changing behavior
_____ yields only _____
results.

2. _____ is not the alternative to
abandoning a system of reward and punishment.

3. Children _____ trained without
the use of threat and punishment.

4. _____ consequences distinguish
between the deed and the doer.

5. Consequences can become _____ if
the teacher becomes upset and personally involved.

6. A teacher must be firm as well as kind in
any pupil-teacher relationship if _____
is to exist between them.

7. A teacher should strive to _____
rather than dominate her class.

8. We can easiest define the four goals of
misbehavior in children under the age of
_____.

9. To be most effective group discussion periods should be _____.

10. We must first change _____ attitude if we expect to succeed in solving any
conflict.

11. Rather than struggling with untrained children we should spend more time training them to _____ in group life.

12. A sociometric test is a good tool for a teacher to use to help her _____ and _____ subgroups.

13. The key characteristic of a sociometric test is that it must be _____ and within the realm of reality.

14. _____ should be encouraged to join extroverted groups so that they have an opportunity to develop socializing skills.

15. Because group relationships change throughout the year a teacher should _____ the sociometric test procedures several times.

chapter 10
The class discussion period

1. The whole class should be involved in helping the problem child in their midst because
_____.
   (a) he is a problem for the whole class
   (b) he is a problem for the teacher
   (c) he deserves our help
   (d) he must improve his written assign-
       ments

2. It is more advantageous for the teacher if
she uses the cooperation of the class members
for _____ than her own authority.

3. By using the group the teacher avoids a
_____ with the misbehaving child.

4. The educational process is _____.
   (a) pleasant
   (b) group-centred
   (c) teacher-centred
   (d) continuous

5. The discussion should be (spontaneous/
structured into the weekly timetable).

6. A particularly beneficial aspect of the
discussion period is that _____.
   (a) it gives the teacher a break period
   (b) it gives the pupils an opportunity to
       solve their own problems
   (c) it stops pupils bothering the teacher
       at recess
   (d) it teaches the pupils patience

7. When class discussion periods are first introduced to the group, initially, the teacher (should/should not) be the chairman.

8. It is the _____ responsibility to confront any misbehaving pupil with his mistaken goals.
    (a) pupil's
    (b) teacher's
    (c) group's
    (d) chairman's

9. A group discussion with confrontation is valuable for all group members because _____.
    (a) it makes some pupils feel more confident about themselves
    (b) it makes some pupils feel good to see someone else put down
    (c) it makes a good addition to the language program
    (d) it allows the teacher to gain more control

10. With regard to the theme of the text, group discussions serve which three of the following purposes:
    (a) to provide practice in oral speaking
    (b) to help children learn to listen
    (c) to negate the possibility of confrontation
    (d) to help children understand themselves
    (e) to stimulate children to help one another
    (f) to provide a forum in which the teacher can air her grievances

11. Group discussions are more effective in changing behavior than individual instruction because _____.
    (a) they give the weaker pupil an opportunity to participate
    (b) they give the successful pupil an opportunity to participate
    (c) they give each member an opportunity to participate
    (d) they give the teacher an opportunity to participate

12. _____ can only be changed in a group.

13. We must establish a congenial _____
if we expect a successful group discussion.

14. The first step for a successful group discussion is _____.
      (a) to understand what each thinks
      (b) to listen to each other
      (c) to have a good chairman
      (d) to tell the other members as much as
          you can

chapter 11
Typical problems and their solutions

1. Dreikurs and Cassel suggest two techniques for reversing a very negative trend in education. By using the two techniques of diagnosing the _____ and _____ the class, teachers would improve classroom behavior immeasurably and thus teaching in general.

2. We will most likely discover the child's mistaken goal by _____.
    (a) threatening to punish him if he does not tell
    (b) promising to give him a candy bar if he tells
    (c) confrontation and observation
    (d) being very pleasant and complimentary

3. The teacher's immediate reaction to a child's misbehavior (is/is not) important to the success of correcting the behavior.

4. If a child deliberately drops her pencil on the floor about five minutes after beginning her arithmetic lesson, the teacher should _____.
    (a) ignore the incident
    (b) reprimand the child
    (c) confront the child with the four goals
    (d) wait until recess then quietly and calmly confront the child with the four goals

5. Whenever a child seeks attention (Goal 1) the teacher should _____.
    (a) confront the child immediately

(b) wait until he gets the pupil alone to confront him or do so at the class discussion period
(c) give immediate attention to the child
(d) not compliment the child when he or she demands it

6. A child who feels accepted and is part of the group will most likely never _____.
    (a) be a problem child
    (b) need attention
    (c) do poorly in school
    (d) be an unhappy child

7. The teacher's emotional reaction to a child's misbehavior is probably the most accurate clue to the child's mistaken goal. Sometimes when you are observing in a classroom (or "observing" yourself) you may hear the teacher say things similar to those listed below. See if you can determine the child's goal [(a) attention, (b) power, (c) revenge, (d) inadequacy from the teacher's reaction indicated by each of the following statements.] (Answer a, b, c, or d.)
    (1) "Stop that, you're starting to annoy me." _____
    (2) "I don't know what to do with you. I give up!" _____
    (3) "OK, who's the boss around here?" _____
    (4) "I can't do a thing with that kid. Nothing will make him do his work." _____
    (5) "How can she be so mean?" _____
    (6) "I don't want to tell you again. Stop tapping your pencil!" _____
    (7) "Who does he think he is? He can't do this to me." _____
    (8) "I'll get him for that." _____
    (9) "I wish she would stop pestering me every recess." _____
    (10) "Get down to the office. You've had it now." _____

8. When dealing with any problem child you must be kind, but you must also be _____

-39-

9. Once the teacher discovers that her problem child is a tyrant struggling for power she should _____.
     (a) admit defeat openly
     (b) admit defeat inwardly
     (c) admit defeat openly and inwardly
     (d) never admit defeat and persevere

10. Any problem child should be shown that there (are/are not) alternatives to his present behavior.

chapter 12
Examples that stopped the tears

1.   The book <u>Discipline Without Tears</u> has been designed primarily to help _____.
   (a) school teachers
   (b) parents
   (c) camp counsellors
   (d) anyone involved with the training of children

2.   A child (can/cannot) be operating toward more than one goal at a time.

3.   Learning through logical consequences usually results in a _____ change in behavior.

4.   Severe spelling problems usually indicate that a child has little respect for _____.
   (a) his parents
   (b) his teacher
   (c) order
   (d) language

5.   One of the most effective ways to help a problem child is to encourage his peers to help him; however, those who help must _____ to do it.

6.   Consensus means a (majority vote/unanimous agreement).

7.   As group awareness increases the teacher will most likely find _____ decreasing.

8. Teachers who are unaware of a misbehaving child's mistaken goal tend to _____ that goal by their reaction to the child's attention-seeking devices.

9. All behaviors, good or bad, of children under ten years of age are directed toward the _____ in order to gain significance.
    (a) group
    (b) adult
    (c) child himself
    (d) class assignments

10. A power-drunk child usually feels that he has to _____ and _____ leadership in order to belong.

11. In a cooperative atmosphere _____.
    (a) everyone behaves properly
    (b) students are more willing to learn
    (c) anarchy exists
    (d) a tyrant thrives

12. Every teacher must provide the _____ for the growth of children's learning, creativity, and potential.

general review

Which of the following major themes are empha-
sized in <u>Discipline Without Tears</u>?

1. In order to find their place in the group,
problem children deliberately misbehave.

2. Permissiveness, which allows the child to
express his needs freely, will stop misbehavior.

3. Recognition of human equality is an essential basis for solving conflict situations.

4. Misbehaving children are operating on a
system of faulty logic.

5. Children's misbehavior is random and indis-
criminate.

6. Both pupils and teachers need to be trained
in democratic methods.

7. We must find new ways of dealing with each
other.

8. Problems arise in the classroom because
society has become so soft.

9. There are a limited and specific number of
mistaken goals that cause conflict situations.

10. To most effectively deal with children
teachers must become democratic leaders.

11. Why most children in our society rebel.

12.   Behavior problems in the classroom are caused by cultural predicaments rather than personal maladjustment.

13.   Regularly scheduled class discussions train children in the methods of participatory democracy.

14.   The diagnosis and treatment of misbehavior in young children is fairly simple.

15.   We must learn to encourage children.

answers to the exercises

CHAPTER 1
1. (b)   2. (c)   3. (d)   4. (a)   5. (d)
6. generate   7. autocratic, arrogance
8. punishing, discouraging   9. Equally as, as
10. does have   11. well organized   12. problem   13. permissive, autocratic, both, responsibilities   14. read, write, compute/do arithmetic   15. democratic   16. exerts, without,
right, within   17. (a), (c), (f), (g), (i),
(j)

CHAPTER 2
1. (c)   2. most   3. punitive, permissive
4. responsibility   5. (c)   6. Discipline
7. free choice   8. (b)   9. can   10. freedom, responsibility   11. does not have
12. (d)   13. become free   14. (a), (d), (e),
(f), (h), (j)   15. (b)   16. can   17. (d)

CHAPTER 3
1. (c)   2. should not   3. (d)   4. (b),
(c), (e)   5. (h)   6. Every   7. (c)
8. make adjustments, cope with problems
9. (a)   10. is   11. attitude   12. may
13. is not   14. all   15. should, although,
can   16. (b)   17. attitude, behavior

REVIEW OF CHAPTERS 1-3
1. autocratic   2. criticizing, punishing
3. (a), (d)   4. all   5. internal stimulation
6. responsibility   7. learning   8. problem-
solving   9. mental health   10. growth and
development   11. preschool   12. attitude
13. goal   14. faulty logic   15. more than
one goal

CHAPTER 4
1. an innate capacity   2. is not, as much an effect   3. (d)   4. faulty logic   5. (a)
6. ten years   7. cannot   8. (c)   9. motivation   10. (d)   11. (b)   12. (c)
13. can, should

CHAPTER 5
1. is not, does not help   2. is not   3. (b)
4. noncompetitive   5. (a), (c), (e), (g), (h),
(i)   6. (a)   7. can   8. democratic
9. human being

CHAPTER 6
1. (d)   2. courage   3. (b)   4. (c)
5. can   6. (a) improvement; (b) efforts, results; (c) strengths; (d) skill; (e) encouragement   7. (c)   8. personal worth   9. discouraging   10. (a)   11. self-centered
12. (b), (c), (e)   13. way or tone of voice
14. (Column B): (g), (e), (a), (c), (b)
15. success   16. Frustration, discouragement

REVIEW OF CHAPTERS 4-6
1. discouraged   2. change the behavior
3. misbehaves, faulty logic   4. attention getting, power, revenge, inadequacy   5. goal
6. noncompetitive   7. competition   8. democratic   9. long-range, temporary   10. human beings   11. avoid   12. all   13. Praise
14. what, way   15. success

CHAPTER 7
1. punishment   2. (c)   3. detrimental
4. is not   5. (b)   6. discouragement
7. cooperation   8. (d)   9. natural, logical
10. (a), (b), (b), (c)   11. (b), (e), (f),
(h)   12. the child   13. (b)   14. Consequences

CHAPTER 8
1. firm   2. (b)   3. (c), (e)   4. inevitable, unavoidable   5. the tyrant   6. (c)
7. mutual respect   8. under ten   9. agree
10. (a)   11. our own   12. (c)

CHAPTER 9
1. (b)   2. prejudice   3. is not   4. is not
5. cohesiveness   6. sociometric test

7. diagnostic   8. (d)   9. (c)   10. socializing   11. (c)   12. change

REVIEW OF CHAPTERS 7-9
1. punishment, temporary   2. Permissiveness
3. can be   4. Logical   5. futile punishment
6. mutual respect   7. influence   8. ten
9. regularly scheduled   10. our own   11. socialize   12. understand, integrate   13. meaningful   14. Isolates   15. repeat

CHAPTER 10
1. (a)   2. behavior correction   3. personal
conflict   4. (d)   5. structured into the
weekly timetable   6. (b)   7. should   8. (b)
9. (a)   10. (b), (d), (e)   11. (c)
12. Values   13. group atmosphere   14. (b)

CHAPTER 11
1. four goals of misbehavior, integrating
2. (c)   3. is   4. (a)   5. (d)   6. (a)
7. (1) a; (2) d; (3) b; (4) d; (5) c; (6) c;
(7) b; (8) c; (9) a; (10) c   8. firm   9. (c)
10. are

CHAPTER 12
1. (d)   2. can   3. permanent   4. (c)
5. volunteer   6. unanimous agreement
7. problems   8. reinforce   9. (b)   10. control, challenge   11. (b)   12. optimum environment

GENERAL REVIEW
1, 3, 4, 6, 7, 9, 10, 12, 13, 14